Fidele Dirokpa Balufuga

History of the Anglican Church of the Congo from its origins to the present day

Fidele Dirokpa Balufuga

History of the Anglican Church of the Congo from its origins to the present day

ScienciaScripts

Imprint

Any brand names and product names mentioned in this book are subject to trademark, brand or patent protection and are trademarks or registered trademarks of their respective holders. The use of brand names, product names, common names, trade names, product descriptions etc. even without a particular marking in this work is in no way to be construed to mean that such names may be regarded as unrestricted in respect of trademark and brand protection legislation and could thus be used by anyone.

Cover image: www.ingimage.com

This book is a translation from the original published under ISBN 978-3-8416-1832-0.

Publisher:
Sciencia Scripts
is a trademark of
Dodo Books Indian Ocean Ltd. and OmniScriptum S.R.L publishing group

120 High Road, East Finchley, London, N2 9ED, United Kingdom
Str. Armeneasca 28/1, office 1, Chisinau MD-2012, Republic of Moldova, Europe
Printed at: see last page
ISBN: 978-620-3-25565-2

Table of contents:

HISTORY OF THE ANGLICAN CHURCH OF CONGO
From the origins to the present day.
By
Dr DIROKPA BALUFUGA Fidèle

DEDICATION

In memory of Mgr Michael Scott-Joynt, Bishop of Winchester, for his enormous assistance to the Anglican Church of Congo (EAC): his friendship and spiritual and pastoral support to EAC leaders, as well as his considerable advocacy in the House of Lords (British Parliament), where he often drew the government's attention to atrocities and injustices during the war years in the Democratic Republic of Congo (DRC).

The Diocese of Winchester (England), which is in partnership with the Church of Uganda, had designated its *Jersey Deanery* to establish a partnership with the EAC. Each EAC diocese is thus twinned with one or more parishes in the Deanery of Jersey (British Channel Island).

ACKNOWLEDGEMENTS

The preparation of this work required the collaboration of a number of individuals and legal entities, as well as various written works. We would like to express our gratitude to them, even if they will not find their names in the list below.

We had the opportunity to meet eminent resource persons such as the first Congolese Anglican priests, Reverends Asani Kabarole and JusuiU Limenya, then Thomas Ndahura, etc., who were Apolo Kivebulaya's catechists and other people who frequented the latter. We also had several opportunities to meet the first retired Archbishop of the Church of Uganda, Burundi, RWANDA and Mboga-Congo, Leslie Wilfrid Brown, as well as the first Bishop of the DIOCESE of Mboga- Congo, Philip Ridsdale and his wife Lucy, who had largely contributed to the writing of the book "African Saint, The Story of Apolo Kivebulaya", Ven. Canon Munege Kabarole, Archdeacon of Bunia, etc. Our conversations about Anglicanism have been a real and consistent source of information and training for us about this Church too. This information has been enriched and completed by our university studies. May they receive our sincere thanks, posthumously, in their place of eternal rest.

Our sincere thanks also to all those who agreed to read this work and who gave me much encouragement throughout the writing of the *History of the Anglican Church of the Congo.* I'd like to mention a few of them here: Reverend Father David Vignot, Mgr Pierre Walon who also prefaced this work, Judy Rous, head of Congo Church Association (CCA), Reverend Venerable Jacques Atoko and Venerable Jean Marie Kithoko Kabange. Many thanks for their dedication and love, as well as for their encouragement, advice, comments, etc. in this work.

From the bottom of our hearts, we extend our sincere thanks to the eminent University Professors who gave up their time to read, correct and guide this work, in particular Dr Valérien Dhedya Bungande, Docteur ès Lettres et Sciences Humaines, Professeur ordinaire à l'Université de Kisangani and Dr Jacques Usungo, Docteur en Histoire et Professeur à l'institut Supérieur Pédagogique de BUKAVU, who read this work with the true professionalism of a proven historian.

Our thanks also go to all the bishops and heads of departments and other people who kindly answered our questionnaires, interviews and provided us with certain documents to help us with this work, etc. May they all receive our sincere gratitude.

Our sincere thanks also go to my family, my wife, my children and other acquaintances, who have supported and encouraged us, morally, spiritually and financially, throughout the writing process, for a truly successful outcome.

May all those who have contributed, from near or far, and who have supported, in one way or another, this scientific work, all find here our feelings of gratitude and may God bless you.

Fai in Kinshasa, October 17, 2016.

++ Dr Dirokpa BalufUga Fidèle

Archbishop Emeritus of the Anglican Church of Congo.

PREFACE

Preface to *"L'HISTOIRE DE L'ÉGLISE ANGLICANE DU CONGO: Des ses origines à nos jours"*, by Monseigneur Fidèle Dirokpa Balufuga.

The Anglican Communion is now the third largest church in the world, with some 90 million members. Although it is often associated with the Church of England alone, the originator of this worldwide Christian phenomenon, English is no longer the *Ungua franca*. The Anglo-Saxon culture of the first missionaries, from Great Britain or the Episcopal Church based in the USA, is no longer the rule. The "average Anglican" is said to be a woman of color, under thirty, who doesn't speak English. Spanish, Portuguese and Swahili are among the languages used in many countries with Anglican churches and dioceses.

And French too. There are currently four million French-speaking Anglicans in the world. The majority of the Anglican churches that cradle them were not founded by Anglo-Saxons. On the contrary, they were evangelized and founded by missionaries from other Anglican churches.

This is the case of the Anglican Church of Congo. At the end of the 19ᵉ century, a Ugandan, Apolo Kivebulaya, walked from Toro (Uganda) to Mboga (Congo) to preach the gospel, teach the Christian faith and train Anglican evangelists. From this spiritual seed, as small as a mustard seed, the great Church we know today has grown.

Monseigneur Fidèle Dirokpa Balufuga, Archbishop Emeritus of the Anglican Church of the Congo and Doctor of Theology from Laval University in Quebec/Canada, has taken on the grandiose task of writing its history. A fine connoisseur of his subject, the Archbishop writes in a fine, uncluttered style, bringing the past to life with a view to the future. What the reader will discover in *L'HISTOIRE DE L'ÉGLISE ANGLICANE DU CONGO* is a marvelous epic, full of suffering and martyrs, but also, like a red thread, magnificent testimonies to the lives of saints formed by the Church of the Congo. With meager means, often suffering from not being English-speaking, through fierce colonial oppression, endless wars and abortive revolutions, Congolese Anglicans have nevertheless erected parishes, charities, schools, Universities, and twelve dioceses, now in both Congo.

In addition to Christian readers, who will draw great inspiration from it, historians and other academic specialists will find in this work a rich source of stories and data. For this work is unprecedented: no one has ventured into it before Bishop Dirokpa. The entire history of the country is scarcely known, and so *HISTOIRE DE L'ÉGLISE ANGLICANE DU CONGO* will be a must-read for a long time to come for all those who hope to learn about the past of this enormous country.

In the future, economists and futurologists predict, the Democratic Republic of Congo and the Republic of Congo will together form the beating heart of the Africa that is becoming the center of the world economy. With extraordinary natural wealth, a people increasingly better educated thanks to the efforts of the churches, and a central geographical position, the two Congos are set for tremendous growth in the years to come.

This requires first and foremost a popular moral foundation, the groundwork for which is currently being laid by the Congolese churches in particular.

And at the forefront of these is the Anglican Church of Congo. Alongside the Roman Catholic Church, it leads the "Peace in the Great Lakes" campaign, which works to bring peace to eastern Congo and neighboring countries. The Church offers medical and spiritual care to women victims of sexual abuse, a weapon of war used by invading rebels. It provides invaluable help to refugees fleeing political instability in their own countries. Its credibility with the Congolese people is solid, having been earned through decades of sustained effort.

Anyone wanting to get a glimpse of the future of this great country would do well to read and study *THE HISTORY OF THE ANGLICAN CHURCH OF CONGO*.

Bishop Pierre Whalon

Bishop in charge of the Episcopal Churches in Europe

President of the French-speaking network of the Anglican Communion

FOREWORD

In order to follow the history of the Anglican Church "Ecclesia Anglicana", the Church of England, in the Democratic Republic of the Congo, a French-speaking state, we feel it is necessary to first briefly explain to laymen, and even to the majority of Congolese Anglicans who do not master their history, what "Anglicanism" is, from its origins at the beginning of the French-speaking world, to briefly explain to laymen, and even to the majority of Congolese Anglicans who have not mastered their history, what "Anglicanism" is, from its origins in England and the various twists and turns it has gone through to become today an international and universal Church.

This historical journey also aims to explain how this Church of the English was introduced into Africa, and more specifically into the Democratic Republic of Congo.

INTRODUCTION

History, the science of learning about the human past, analyzes the origins and evolution of events through the ages. It also highlights the characters or actors who have influenced the course of events in one way or another, as well as their works and their impact. To achieve this, it is always essential to base analyses on irrefutable evidence gleaned from everywhere, such as photographic illustrations or other irrefutable proofs.

As the memory of humanity or of any group, history is only useful when it informs and educates posterity on an important subject that concerns them. Such is the case with the history of the Anglican Church of the Congo, which should provide information on the origins, evolution and impact of this religious community in the Democratic Republic of the Congo.

Unfortunately, the Anglican Church of the Congo, which will celebrate its 120^e anniversary this year, does not yet have a large-scale document containing its history in a single, easy-to-consult compendium. Of course, we have history books written by the missionaries about Apolo Kivebulaya and its activities (1896-1933), as well as about the era of the European missionaries (1933-1960). But after the Democratic Republic of Congo gained independence, the Anglican Church came under the leadership of national officials, and there are still no history books on the Anglican Church of Congo, covering the long 56-year period from 1960 to 2016. Only the rudiments of this Church's history can be found in doctoral theses, undergraduate and graduate dissertations, articles in magazines, newspapers or other publications, pamphlets, etc., which does not always satisfy those who would really like to know the history of Anglicanism, because it is only a part of the history that is presented. In this book, we have attempted to bring together a variety of historical information from different sources in a single document, which will be easy to consult for those interested in the history of the Anglican Church in the Congo.

To avoid the hazards associated with the distortion of historical accounts by the wear and tear of memory, and the disappearance of traces following the death of actors and witnesses, the efficient preservation of historical facts is generally achieved through writing and engraving on magnetic and other media. It is for this reason that we have decided to write the history of the Anglican Church of Congo, in order to provide present and future generations with essential data on this religious community.

History is the school of life, they say. It presents us with examples to imitate and experiences to avoid. In the specific case of the history book of the Anglican Church of Congo, it enables readers to :

- Explain the origins, evolution and impact of this Church through the various stages of its history, in order to consider ways and means of moving forward;
- Analyze the work accomplished by the pioneers and seek to do the same, with a view to better implanting the Anglican community in every nook and cranny of the Democratic Republic of Congo;
- Mastering Anglican history to correct past errors or weaknesses: to stimulate common commitment within the Church;
- To make available to members of the Anglican Community of Congo and elsewhere, researchers and the curious from all horizons, an easy consultation tool, available in the various Dioceses, parishes scattered across the country, libraries or other places where works and archives are kept.

The history of the Anglican Church in the Congo is divided into two main periods. Each epoch is further subdivided into two periods, each spanning, more or less, some thirty years:

First Era: *The Anglican Church of Mboga: From missionary leadership to Congo's independence (1896-1960)*

A. Apolo Kivebulaya (1896-1933) and the establishment of the Anglican Church in the Belgian Congo

B. European missionaries and the consolidation of Apolo Kivebulaya's work (1933-1960)

Second Era: *The Anglican Church of Congo under the leadership of Congolese Officials (1960-2016)*

A. Essor de l'Eglise anglicane du Congo: de l'indépendance au centenaire de l'implantation de l'Eglise (1960-1996)

B. The influence of evangelical works after the centenary (1996-2016)

In compiling this book, we have drawn on a number of reliable sources and resources: dioceses, partners, books, published and unpublished works, archives, leaflets, interviews, iconographic documents, our personal experiences, etc. Its sole aim is to provide the Anglican Church of the Congo with a solid historical document with which to be itself, feeling at ease in discussions, teachings, providing information to others, etc.

ANGLICANISM

1. Etymology

To understand "Anglicanism in Africa", one must first master "the Church of England", because Anglicanism is intimately linked to the history of the Church of England. The terms "Anglican"(1) and "Anglicanism " are derived from the Latin word *Anglicanus*, meaning *English* and translated into French as "English". The name *Ecclesia Anglorum* (Church of the English) comes from Pope Gregory the Great, who used it in his letter to his bishop Augustine of Canterbury, around the beginning of the 5th century. The name *Ecclesia Angliae* (Church of England) dates back to the time of Anselm of Canterbury towards the end of the 11th century.

The expression *Ecclesia Anglicana* had been commonly used in correspondence since the middle of the 12th century. It was translated into English as Church of England.

As for the term "Anglican", it refers to a "tribalization" of the faith, since it originally meant "English". In this sense, Anglicanism is nothing other than the expression of the Holy Catholic and Apostolic Church in English culture. Spirituality, worship, Bible-reading, etc., all bear the hallmarks of English culture, which, incidentally, are not necessarily familiar to the African man.

Consequently, the name "Eglise Anglicane du Congo" simply means "Church of the English in the Congolese environment". As far as Congolese Anglicanism is concerned, we speak of "L'Eglise anglicane du Congo" and not of "Eglise anglicane au Congo". The use of the denomination "Anglican" and of the contracted article "<u>du</u>" instead of the preposition "<u>au</u>", was decided by the Executive Council of the Anglican Church of Congo held in 1992 in Bunia, at the time when the aforementioned Council was discussing the change of name of the Anglican Church to Episcopal Church . The idea is that it is not the Church of the English that is being transferred to the Congo, but rather a Congolese Church that shares the doctrine of the Church as interpreted by the Anglican Reformation. In fact, in many countries affected by Anglicanism, the expression " Anglican Church " is used to erase the connotation of a foreign Church, especially an English one .
Anglicanism, as argued by Canon Jacques Brossière (2). What the Congolese call the " EgliseanglicaneduCongo ", is also known as the " EgliseEpiscopaledes USA", "Eglise Episcopale du Soudan", "Eglise Episcopale du Rwanda", "Eglise Episcopale du Brésil", "Eglise Episcopale d'Haïti", and so on. In England, the Church is not called the Anglican Church, but the Church of England, as well as the Church of Uganda, the Church of India and so on. In Japan, Anglicanism is called "The Holy Catholic Church of Japan". Despite this diversity of names, all members of Anglicanism recognize themselves as Anglicans.

So, while Anglicanism originally concerned only the Church of England, since the development of the Anglican Communion with the colonial imperialism of the XVIII[e] century, Anglicanism is no longer identified with the history of England. Nevertheless, it has managed to preserve its tradition and spread throughout the world.

2. The Anglican Communion

It is a group of national or regional Churches, also called "Provinces" [Ecclesiastical, with a primate Archbishop at the head], whose succession of bishops has its origins in the early Church through the Church of England. These provinces, gathered around the See of Canterbury, are in communion with each other, and it is the Archbishop of Canterbury who exercises the ministry of presidency at their head. He symbolizes the unity, union and cohesion of the Anglican Church worldwide.

There are currently 38 provinces [Ecclesiastical with Primate Archbishops at the head] and over 90 million Anglicans, including over 4 million French-speaking Anglicans, spread across some 165 countries out of 192 countries on the globe.

Regarding the origins of the "Anglican Communion" (3), it has to be said that Christianity has existed in Great Britain since the Isle of Man. Christian remains dating back to the second century AD have just been found. The young, flourishing British Church sent representatives to the Council of Arles (southern France) in 319 AD.

Following the conquest of the country by the pagan Anglo-Saxons from northern Europe, England had benefited from a new Roman missionary impetus, notably the sending of monks by Pope Gregory the Great (590-604). Among these was Saint Augustine, consecrated bishop in 597, who became the first Archbishop of Canterbury in 601.

Following the Norman invasion of 1066, William the Conqueror, now king, refused to pay homage to the Pope. He appointed French bishops of his own choosing to all important posts. This tradition of independence pitted the King against the Pope for control of the Church, and continued throughout the Middle Ages. An anticlerical sentiment gradually took hold and developed strongly, due to the excessive privileges granted to this category of Church ministers. In particular, the payment of tithes to Rome, the right to appeal to Rome and the clergy's immunity under civil law were contested.

3. The Anglican Reformation in the 16th century
3.1. Henry VIII's schism (1534-1547): Catholicism without a Pope

A study of the motives behind the complete break with Rome in 1538, during the reign of Henry VIII, reveals that this event had no real bearing on the creation of a new Church in England. Rather, the break with Rome should be seen as an affirmation of the right of the English to regulate their own affairs, since Church and State were inseparable at that time. It should also be noted that the Church had long exercised great influence over the life of the nation, and the Pope, through the system of "excommunication", was able to incite Christians to revolt against their political authorities. So the idea of having a Catholic Church of England independent of Rome had been present in the English mindset for a long time.

In England, the break was due first and foremost to the will of King Henry VIII. Indeed, King Henry VIII's marriage was merely an incident or opportunity, albeit an inappropriate one, to declare the divorce of the Catholic Church of England from the Catholic Church of Rome. The causes were many and varied, as noted above. The divorce from Rome was supported by Martin Luther's reformation against medieval indulgence thinking, and John Wyclif's anti-papal movement against land expropriation and Rome's attempts to dominate other nations through the Roman Catholic Church. It is clear from the above that the King's divorce was only a pretext, not the primary cause of the rupture. To the reasons cited above, we must add the king's desire to have a male heir to the throne, as all the children he had by his wife Catherine of Aragon were dying at an early age.

Theologians believe they can find the explanation for this phenomenon in the Bible, specifically in the Book of Leviticus 20:21, and encouraged King Henry XVIII to ask the Pope to declare his marriage [not divorce] with Catherine of Aragon null and void.

As Pope Clement VII could not think of upsetting King Charles V, his protector and nephew of Catherine of Aragon, he did not hasten to make a decision. So Henry VIII proclaimed himself *"Supreme Head after Christ of the Church of England"* in 1531. This declaration was ratified by Parliament with the Act of Supremacy in 1534, which made the King the sole Supreme Head on earth of the Church of England: *Ecclesia Anglicana* or *Church of England*. And now he and his advisors could freely divorce and remarry Ann Boleyn.

Ultimately, the Church of England sees itself as the traditional Church of the English nation, purged of all medieval error and no longer subordinate to papal authority, but in continuity with the ancient Church. Indeed, while retaining the apostolic ministry, the Church submits to royal authority.

It believed itself to be truly Catholic, but tended to identify with Protestantism in its struggle against the forces of the Counter-Reformation. Henry VIII thus established the Anglican Church in a kind of "Middle Way" [Via Media], between the Catholic and Protestant Churches.

After the king's death in 1547, the Church's revolution continued in turmoil, as each king adopted a different course of action from his predecessor.

3.2. The Protestant offensive under Edward VI (1547-1553)

Edward VI acceded to the throne of England at the age of 9. During his minority, the government was in the hands of a regency whose most influential leaders were Protestant. In agreement with his advisors, he left Henry VIII's "Middle Way" and adopted the Lutheran theses his father had fiercely opposed. The marriage of priests was thus permitted. Archbishop Thomas Cranmer was able to reveal his reforming soul, and in 1549, with the help of a commission of theologians, he published "The Book of Common Prayer", the official document of worship whose use was imposed throughout the kingdom by *the "Act of Uniformity"*. Unlike the Roman Catholics, from now on a single Book replaced the breviary, missal, book of customs, etc. It was intended for clergy and priests alike. It is intended for both clergy and faithful. It is written in the local language, enabling everyone to follow the services.

3.3.   **The uncompromising Catholicism of Mary Tudor (1553-1558)**

During the short-lived reign of Mary Tudor (daughter of Henry VIII and Catherine of Aragon), the old link with the Pope was re-established. The kingdom was returned to the Catholic faith. The clergy ordained according to Cranmer's liturgy had their pastoral duties taken away from them. The Catholic faith and the Mass were restored. Mary Tudor was also known as "*Mary the Bloody*", because all those who refused to submit to papal authority were to be burned alive at the stake; and once the stake was lit, the fire never went out for the 5 years of her reign.

3.4.   **Elizabeth Iere and the Anglican compromise (1558-1603)**

Under the reign of Elizabeth Iere to the throne, the definitive break with Rome took place. The Church of England and its new doctrine were permanently established by an Act of Parliament and fully integrated into the legislation and structures of the regime. Henceforth, the foundation of faith was no longer the leaders of the Church, but the sovereign with his Parliament. *The Book of Common Prayer* and Cranmer's ordination ritual were revived. The Queen also reinstated the Act of Supremacy and regained her title as *Supreme Head, on earth, of the Church of England, a* title held by the kings or queens of England to this day. But this applies to England only. The Queen also set up a new hierarchy, since all but one of the bishops had refused the oath of supremacy.

In 1588, *the "invincible Armada",* an immense Spanish war fleet organized by the Pope, attempted to convince England by force of arms to return to "the true Church". The crushing defeat of this invasion laid the foundations of the modern English state and represented the final stage in the rift between Rome and Canterbury, a rift that was to remain almost absolute until the Second Vatican Council (5).

However, significant contact between the Church of England and the Church of Rome did not take place until after the Second Vatican Council (1963), when Pope John XXIII recognized the specificity of the Anglican Church, declaring that "*of all the Churches separated from Rome, this one remains the closest to the Roman Catholic Church*".

Indeed, the Anglican Reformation of the 16th^e century, as we said, was not a new beginning; it in no way represented the establishment of a new Church, other than the Apostolic. While it rejected the authority of the Pope, it retained doctrine, liturgy and vestments, the sacraments and ecclesiastical orders: the diaconate, the priesthood/presbyterate and the episcopate. Anglicanism has always affirmed itself as both a Catholic and a Reformed Church. It has taken a "Middle Way" [Via Media]. There is no specifically Anglican theological doctrine, as there was for Martin Luther, John Calvin or Ulrich Zwingli.

The Anglican Church teaches all the doctrines of the Catholic faith as expressed in the Apostles' Creed, the Nicene Creed, the Ecumenical Councils and the writings of the Church Fathers, which preceded the split between East and West in 1054 [between Constantinople and Rome]. In other words, the authority of its doctrine rests on 3 pillars: Sacred Scripture, Tradition and Reason. This differs from other Protestant churches, for whom only the Holy Scriptures (*Sola Scriptura*) form the basis of faith. It is this national Church of the English, having gone through a long period of Reformation, from which it emerged well structured and organized doctrinally, culturally, administratively, hierarchically, etc., that will become, without conscious effort, a worldwide Communion.

4. The expansion of the Anglican Church outside Britain
4.1.   The era of Chaplaincies and Missionary Societies

Following the explorations undertaken by the English, which were to lead to the establishment of the British Empire in the XVIIIeme and XIXeme centuries, Chaplaincies were opened for sailors on expedition ships and in the ports where they were stationed. At first, Anglican worship was only available to these English sailors. It was only later that the Gospel was preached to the natives, to those living in the vicinity of the ports, and then to the interior of the Continent.

After this stage, the Missionary Societies go into action to send missionaries to new fields of evangelization.

Examples include the Church Missionary Society (C.M.S.) in London, founded in 1799, and the United Society for the Propagating of the Gospel (U.S.P.G.).

And if in the early days, according to historical phenomena and circumstances, Anglicanism had particular and intimate links with the state in England, this no longer applies to the present-day Christian denominations that profess Anglicanism in the rest of the world. They have become independent of any external authority and enjoy great freedom, while remaining within the great Anglican family : the   "COMMUNION".
ANGLICANE", a single "body" whose unity persists, to this day, despite diverse tendencies.

In fact, the English gave free rein to an explosive energy that took them to the remotest corners of the earth, where, under the guise of colonial expansion, they brought with them the English language   ,   their administration, their   customs   and their religion
: America, the coasts of Africa towards India, Australia, New Zealand and so on. This was the route by which Anglicanism was also introduced into Africa.

4.2.   The painful beginnings of the Anglican Church in East Africa: Uganda

The first Church Missionary Society (C.M.S.) missionary to East Africa was the German Dr. J.L. Krapf, who arrived in Mombasa in 1844. The following year, he was joined by another German, J. Rebman. The two pioneers held on for a generation, albeit with great difficulty. At the time, there was no sign of the bountiful harvest that would follow in their wake.

Sent to Africa by the American newspapers *The Daily Telegraph* and *New York Herald* to complete the work of David Livingstone, English explorer and journalist Henry Morton Stanley spent several days in Uganda. He was received by Kabaka Mutesa I, King of the Baganda, on April 5, 1875. After convincing the king of the truth of the Christian religion versus the "falsehood" of the Islamic religion, Stanley wrote a letter to London's *Daily Telegraph* on April 14, 1875, asking England to send missionaries to Uganda. Stanley's letter appeared in the newspaper on November 15, 1875. The C.M.S., always a lover of great undertakings, responded favorably to the appeal, and the first detachment of missionaries arrived in Uganda on June 30, 1877. They were received by the Kabaka Mutesa of the Baganda on July 2, 1877. They were Lieutenant Shergold Smith and Reverend C.T. Wilson. There they found Evangelist Maftaa, who had come from Nyassaland, now Malawi, with Stanley, who continued to serve them as interpreter, just as he had done for Stanley.

It is worth noting the contribution of Scottish engineer and teacher Alexander Mackay to the establishment of Anglicanism in Uganda. He arrived at the Royal Court in November 1878. His qualities were soon felt in the community.

Indeed, Alexander Mackay was a pious, practical, courageous and intelligent man. His continual preference for Scripture seems to have made a deep impression on Kabaka Mutesa. For, after his arrival at court, followers eager to learn to read and write were authorized by the king to attend the mission. And the Anglican Church was beginning to take root in the area.

Two years later, the Catholic missionaries White Fathers arrived in Uganda. A kind of rivalry ensued between Anglicans and Catholics, but the English colonial government instinctively placed special trust in the Anglican mission.

From 1885 to 1887, Christians endured harsh suffering and persecution in various parts of Uganda, as Kabaka Mwanga, the new king of the Baganda since 1884, did not want missionaries, who he felt were destroying their customs and traditions. He decided to totally eradicate Christianity from his kingdom. More than 45 Christians had already been martyred in various parts of the kingdom.

James Hannington, the first Anglican bishop for East Africa, was murdered on January 29, 1885 in Kyondo, Busoga, before arriving in Mengo, present-day Kampala, the capital of the Buganda kingdom. From then on, persecution was unleashed against Christian neophytes. On June 3, 1886, 25 young men, including 13 Anglicans and 12 Catholics, were burned at the stake in Namgongo. Rivalries between Roman Catholics and Anglicans had greatly weakened and divided Christians, who nevertheless remained united in a common refusal to offend Christ.

The blood of the martyrs is a true grain of faith for the Church of Uganda *(Sanguis martirum, semen christianorum)*, which then experienced a tremendous explosion on the field of evangelization. It was this Church of Uganda, which had already proven its faith in Jesus Christ, that brought Anglicanism to the Democratic Republic of Congo, a French-speaking country in Central Africa (6), from the town of Mboga.

Notes

(1)   Paul *Avis, What is Anglicanism,* quoted by Dr. Yossa Way, in his doctoral *thesis, La Spiritualité de l'Eglise anglicane du Congo face aux défis contemporains,* Faculté Protestante du Congo, UPC, Kinshasa, 2009, p. 80.

(2) Jacques Bossiere, "L'âme de l'anglicanisme", in *Cahiers de l'Anglicanisme Francophone,* n° 3, 2001, p. 30

"This neologism was coined by Jacques Bossiere and first used in Limuru/Kenya in 1996, at the first global meeting of representatives of French-speaking Anglican dioceses around the world.

(3)   MarcGudwin,   *LaCommunionanglicane   : Unaperçu   pourles*   chrétiens

d'expressionfrançaise, Perspectives épiscopaliennes nol, new edition, Montreal, 1981, p. 2. This little book was used extensively in the section on defining Anglicanism.

(4)   Ibid, p. 2.

(5)   Ibid, p. 3.

(6) Not to be confused with the *Anglican Ecclesiastical Province of Central Africa,* which includes Zambia, Malawi, Botswana and Zimbabwe, and the *11 Central African countries*: Democratic Republic of Congo, Burundi, Congo-Brazzaville, Central African Republic, Chad, Gabon, Cameroon, Angola, Equatorial Guinea, Rwanda and Sao Tomé & Principe.

Part 1
FIRST ERA
THE MBOGA ANGLICAN CHURCH: FROM MISSIONARY LEADERSHIP TO CONGO INDEPENDENCE (1896-1960)
Chapter 1

A. APOLO KIVEBULAYA (1896-1933) AND THE ESTABLISHMENT OF THE ANGLICAN CHURCH IN CONGO BELGE

Those who heard of Apolo Kivebulaya would think he was a highly educated and perhaps very wealthy man. However, this was not the case, and he had no considerable resources, unlike the expatriate missionaries who were endowed with material comforts. In order to better establish themselves and easily win over the population to the new religion, it was necessary, in certain circumstances, to offer gifts to village or clan chiefs. Moreover, at the time of the colonization of Africa, when the black man was demonized, it was hard to imagine such a laudable work being carried out by an African, whatever his intellectual capacity. Against all prejudice, Apolo Kivebulaya succeeded in establishing the first Anglican mission at Mboga, now called "Boga", in the Belgian Congo, now the Democratic Republic of Congo.

It should be pointed out, however, that at the start of Apolo's ministry, Mboga was in Uganda. It was after the first border change in 1911 that the Semliki River became the current border, and since then Mboga has been in the Belgian Congo, now the DRC.

1. About the Democratic Republic of Congo and Mboga
1.1 Democratic Republic of Congo (DRC)

The Democratic Republic of Congo is the second largest country on the African continent after Algeria. Located in the heart of the country, it is eighty times larger than its former metropolis, Belgium, and four times the size of France. All in all, the DRC is the size of Western Europe. The Congolese consider it a subcontinent, as it fits 2.5 times into the Australian continent. It covers an area of 2,345,409 Km .^{2}

Congo's various name changes

Area: 2,345,409 Km^2

Population: 80 million

Languages: over 450, including French, Swahili, Lingala, Tshiluba and Kikongo.

Formerly :
- Independent State of Congo (1885 to 1908)
- Belgian Congo (1908 to 1960)
- Belgian Congo and Ruanda - Urundi (1918-1960)

Independence: June 30, 1960
- De1960a1964   :Republiquedu Congo
- 1964a1971   :DemocraticRepublicofCongo
- De1971a1997   :Republicof   Zaire
- From 1997   : Democratic Republic of Congo

Successively called Etat Indépendant du Congo (1885-1908), Congo Belge (19081960), Republic of Congo (1960-1964), Democratic Republic of Congo (1964-1971), Republic of Zaire (1971-1997) and the Democratic Republic of Congo (DRC) since 1997, this country straddles the equator between latitudes 5°20' North and 13°27' South, and between longitudes 12°15' and 31°15' East. The DRC opens onto the Atlantic Ocean at Moanda/Banana and is bordered by 9 countries: the Republic of Congo (Brazzaville), the Central African Republic, Sudan, Uganda, Rwanda, Burundi, Tanzania, Zambia and Angola.

The Democratic Republic of the Congo is a   country of resources

The region is rich in natural resources, minerals, numerous rivers, a vast equatorial forest and very fertile soil.

According to current estimates, the DRC has a population of over 80 million, a heterogeneous and heteroclite people comprising half a thousand ethnic groups, generally grouped into 4 main groups: the Bantu (the most numerous), the Sudanese, the Nilotics and the Pygmies. The Congolese population speaks a multitude of different languages, although the government has imposed four national languages as *lingua franca*: Swahili, Tshiluba (Ciluba), Lingala and Kikongo, as well as one official language, French.

In religious terms, the Congolese practiced traditional religions before Christianity and Islam were gradually imposed.

1.2 **Mboga locality**

TORO (Uganda) and MBOGA (CONGO) regions, 1894

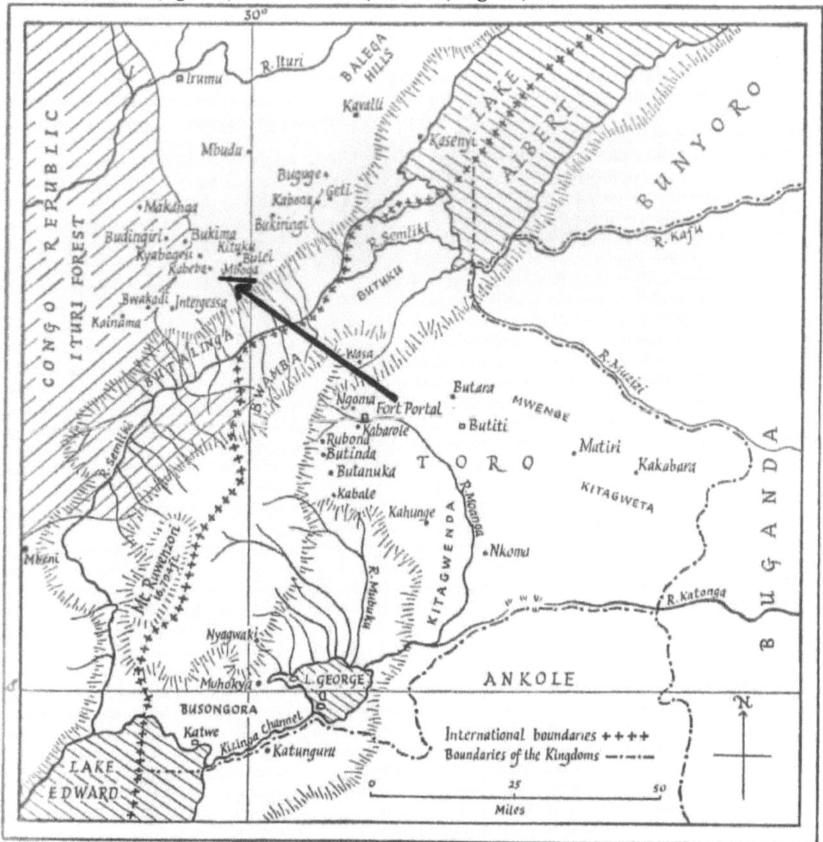

Map in "African Saint: "The story of Apolo Kivebulaya" by Anne Luck, London, SCM Press, 1963, p. 9

Mboga is a small village in Irumu Territory, Ituri Province, in the northeast of the Democratic Republic of Congo. The village lies on the western slopes of the escarpments of *the Rift Valley*, which runs from the Dead Sea to Lake Nyassa (Malawi). This valley forms a large plain containing several lakes and major rivers, including Lake Albert and the Semliki River, between which the town of Mboga lies. The escarpments on the Ugandan side are formed by the Ruwenzori Mountains, with snowfall at its three peaks, also known as *The* Mountains of the Moon. Mboga is inhabited by the Banyamboga people, also known as Bahema. They speak Lunyoro or Kihema, one of Uganda's languages, in the Toro District.

With the exception of the Pygmies (Bambuti), also known as the first inhabitants of Central Africa, all Congo's tribes are the product of immigration.

Anne Luck describes the people of Mboga in the following terms:

"The Mboga (Banyamboga) peoples were originally Bahuma herders, who migrated probably in the second half of the 17th century through the Rift Valley of Mwenge Province, part of Bunyoro. The Mukama Tabaro (king), reigning in 1896 in Boga, was the 17th inductee of this sub-dynasty (...). News of good grazing on the border with the Grand Congo led to three migrations from southern Bunyoro. It is reported that Isingoma forbade intermarriage with neighboring tribes, and to this day the Banyamboga have retained their language and customs, while other immigrants from Bunyoro to the west of Lake Albert had freely intermarried with the Balega and lost their language and customs, though they retained their characteristic features, religion and cow ritual" (1).

1.3 The life of Apolo Kivebulaya

Apolo en 1930

Apolo Kivebulaya, whose real name Waswa (3) was reserved for twins, was born in 1864 to a family of 5 children in Kiwanda, Singo District, in the former kingdom of Buganda (Uganda). His twin brother was called Kato. His father was Samuel Salongo Kisamuzi and his mother Nalongo Tezira. At the age of 15, Waswa (he was not yet Apolo) received Christian influence from a Church Missionary Society (C.M.S.) missionary, Alexander Mackay, who arrived in Uganda in 1878.

Mackay was a pious man, intelligent, courageous and skilled in manual labor. Young Waswa had come to know him at King Mutesa's court, when he wanted to benefit from the missionary's teachings. These included learning to read and teaching the Bible.

On the death of Kabaka Mutesa 1ᵉʳ , his son Mwanga succeeded him in 1884. The latter king persecuted the Christians in favor of the Muslims. He hoped to obtain guns from the missionaries to give him supremacy over rival kingdoms, but unfortunately this was not to be. However, the Arabs who traded in slaves provided him with them and, in gratitude, he rallied to their side. It was under this Kabaka, in October 1885, that the martyrdom of Monsignor James Hannington, the first Anglican missionary bishop sent by the C.M.S. to Equatorial Africa, took place.
than that of   theonescorte .   1886and   1888were
            theyearsofgreatproductionof   the
Christian.

The young Waswa, recognized as a Muslim, was thus forced to enlist in the Islamic army to fight the Christians. However, Islam was not to his liking, because of the wanton slaughter it perpetrated against innocent Christians. Waswa remembered the evangelical teachings and positive attitudes of missionary Alexander Mackay, whom he had known as a child.

Having himself participated in several massacres of Christians, he decided to leave the Islamic army and flee to Ankole, another Ugandan kingdom. There, he made friends with other Anglican Christians and learned the Word of God. Apolo points to Matthew 5:13 as the key verse in his conversion: *"You are the salt of the earth..."*. Back in his native land, he had a strong desire to? become a child of God. So, in 1894, he enrolled in the catechumenate. He was baptized on January 27, 1895, under the name of Apolo. It was then that Waswa received the name Apolo, thus making his entry into the history of the Anglican Church of Congo, right up to the present day. The choice of this first name was motivated by the passage in Acts 18:25: "(...) *being fervent in spirit, he proclaimed and taught accurately the things concerning the Lord*" (2). We see how Apolo's life completely fulfilled this verse. It was his official accession to the Anglican Church. In the meantime, Apolo had been engaged to a girl with whom he attended the catechumenate class. But she died prematurely before the wedding, and Apolo decided not to marry again. Later, in the face of many trials, he realized that his fiancée's untimely death was indeed God's will, as she should have had a hard time in the difficult situations his ministry was about to experience.

To this we must add the *sobriquet Kivebulaya*, which literally means "*something from Europe (England)*" (4) and was given to him in jest because of his attire, which was somewhat different from the usual practice in his milieu at the time. He wore a red jacket (reserved for the military) over a white masculine dress. "*I am full of glory as a soldier of Jesus*", he often said. This jacket was given to him by Major Roddy Owen of the British army. So it was this jacket, when he spoke of what came from Europe, a garment that gave him great pride in his ministry.

Rightly or wrongly, this sobriquet summed up people's idea of Evangelism: what he told, what he taught and the liturgy of the Anglican Church itself were something of the Europe that Apolo had brought to the Congo.

Apolo had thus become a mythical hero in Boga circles, so that even today there are people who resist any change, the reason being that Apolo hadn't taught that, hadn't said that or done that.

This idea of Apolo as a mythical figure has even led to ignoring the merits of other missionaries and servants of God who have worked for the growth of the Anglican Church in the Congo down the ages. Deaconess Lucy and her husband, Bishop Philip Ridsdale, the first Bishop of Mboga, responding to my questionnaires on Apolo's work in November 1998, wrote to me as follows: "Apolo's work was the foundation of the Church in Congo; he had become a Munyamboga, but the living Gospel did not depend on him, but had its root in Christ; that's why it was growing".

So, in practice, the Banyamboga sometimes seemed to give more importance to the person of Apolo than to the action of the Holy Spirit in the Church.

2. Evangelizing Mboga

When the first Ugandan Anglican missionaries arrived in Mboga, no one could expect an easy ministry. In this environment, the natives had never been in contact with the Gospel, and most of their traditional practices were incompatible with the Word of God.

Indeed, in this environment, the consumption of alcoholic beverages was the main leisure activity for both men and women. Fetishism and witchcraft had a dominant influence on the population. Worship of ancestors and benevolent spirits was the only way to conciliate the world of invisible powers. Some people were possessed by evil spirits. Polygamy was in full swing. Slavery was also practiced in Boga (5). People, especially children, were exchanged for various products. The slaves were often forest dwellers whom the Banyamboga put to their service after buying them in exchange for food or land to cultivate. These slaves were used as currency in all transactions. A little further from Mboga, among the Nyali people, cannibalism was practised (6). These were the kind of problems that Apolo Kivebulaya and his collaborators were to face.

Knowing some of the reasons for failure of his predecessors, Apolo, on his journey from Uganda to Mboga, wanted first to solve the vital problem of food subsistence. Continuing on his way to Mboga, as he passed through the forest, he equipped himself with wooden sticks which he foresaw being used as hoe handles to cultivate the field. By this act, Apolo had solved one of the problems that had aroused the natives' distrust of his predecessors. As soon as he arrived, he won the esteem of the chief, who saw in him a man who did not seek to live at the expense of others. For the rest of his life in Mboga, he remained a man committed to working the land to meet the food needs of his visitors and his own, following the example of the Apostle Paul.

2.1 The first period of evangelization (1894)

In 1894, the 12^e king of the Mboga dynasty, Paulo Tabaro II, crossed the Semliki River to visit his newly enthroned colleague, Kasagama de Toro in Uganda, to request British protectorate over his territory. His colleague told him about the religion practiced in his country, which taught people to read and write. Interested by this information, Chief Tabaro sought out Ugandan evangelists and, within a short time, two of them, Petero Nsubuga and Sedulaka Makwata, followed him to Mboga (7). On their arrival in this locality, these two pioneers of Anglicanism were well received by the Tabaro chief and built a chapel near the royal court. However, within a year, the two catechists were forced to leave the area and return to Uganda.

According to Tibenderana Yakobo, they were proud and would not touch the work in the fields, which they felt was reserved for the lower classes, notably women and slaves. What's more, these foreigners refused to take the local alcoholic beverage, which everyone had to consume in the royal court (8). So the chief ordered his subjects to stop feeding these catechists until they left the area.

Some critics believe that these early missionaries were forced to turn back   because   Chief   Tabarole   was   hostile to   them . The new religion would sweep away ancestral customs and, as a result, undermine his kingship.

All in all, Petero Nsubuga and Sedulaka Makwata were forced to leave the mission field because they were unable to adapt to the local culture. They saw themselves as superior to the evangelized.

Although the first evangelization of Mboga gave the impression of failure, this was only apparent, since, despite the departure of the catechists, the Gospel had already touched some hearts and the Church was already established in the area. It was simply necessary to send other, more enterprising catechists to continue the mission. And the choice fell on Apolo Kivebulaya.

2.2 The second evangelization period (1896)

Apolo Kivebulaya, Evangelizer

How beautiful are the feet that preach the Good News of peace (RmlO: 14-15)
Anne Luck, p. 43

The forced desertion of Mboga's first Anglican missionaries did not discourage the Church of Uganda, which sent other catechists to the area.

In August 1896, Rev. A.B. Fisher and A.B. Lloyd visited Mboga, where they found people who were still enthusiastic about future teaching, but the chief wasn't too happy about it. A.B. Fisher wrote: "*We wanted to send a faithful and enduring catechist... so Apolo put himself forward as a candidate*" (9).

With the first seeds of Anglican evangelism for the Congo already sown in Mboga, Apolo Kivebulaya was sent in 1896 to continue the work abandoned by his predecessors.

Having spotted the village of Mboga high up in the Ruwenzori Mountains because of the smoke rising from it in the distance amidst the dense forest, Apolo began to think about bringing the Good News to this distant land.

Apolo was a young convert from Islam who had just been baptized on January 7, 1895, just one year earlier. But he was found sincere and faithful by the ecclesiastical authorities. He had undergone a short biblical training in Namirembe, Kampala.
Hired as a catechist in the year of his baptism, he was sent to work in Toro (Uganda).

Apolo Kivebulaya arrived in Mboga in September 1896, accompanied by Sedulaka, to replace previous catechists who had just returned to Uganda.

As far as the evangelization of Mboga was concerned, the inhabitants of this region had initially shown themselves insensitive to the evangelical message brought by Apolo. The superficial evangelization of his predecessors had not left much of a mark. But in December 1896, through his intense evangelization, Apolo succeeded in enrolling 14 people in the catechumenate. They were baptized in Mboga on April 4, 1897 by Reverend J.S. Callis (10). On August 24, 1898, 7 received confirmation and 13 others were baptized by Bishop Alfred Tucker.

It should be noted that during this period, Mboga was disputed between the Belgian Congo and the British Colony of Uganda. The Mboga region did not return definitively to the Belgian Congo until 1911. As for the Anglican Church of Congo, it continued to depend on the Anglican Church of Uganda in all respects until the 1980s, two decades after Congo's independence in 1960.

3. The trials of the nascent Church

3.1 **The fallout from the Dhanis column revolt and Chief Tabaro's about-face**

The joy of the first harvest was immediately followed by hardship. There was the mutiny of the Force publique de l'Etat indépendant du Congo led by Baron Dhanis (11). The mutineers were ruthless gunmen who stormed the town of Mboga, setting fire to houses and the church. Much property was looted, and women and children were taken hostage.

This misfortune was immediately followed by the untimely death of Chief Tabaro's son. Discouraged, the king ordered a return to the practices of traditional religion, notably that of worshipping the spirits of the ancestors, and publicly confessed that God did not exist. Having been consulted about the origin of these misfortunes, the fetishists and seers claimed that it was due to the presence of the catechists in the village. This further aroused the chief's hatred of the Christians and the young Church. As a result, many Christians were expelled from the royal court. Others simply resigned themselves to the ruler's orders and withdrew from the Church.

The toughest test came in 1898, when the small core of faithful, led by spiritual leader Apolo, decided to build a church. While they were preparing the site, a spear was placed next to the wall of Apolo's house.

Suddenly, they saw the bushfire spring up behind Chief Tabaro's residence. It was the dry season and bushfire was not easy to control.
As the fire approached Apolo's house, it was immediately necessary to start moving the belongings out of the house to save them from a possible fire. Faced with these uncontrolled movements, a young girl, Malyamu Tuguita, sister of the Tabaro chief, fell running onto the spear placed against Apolo's house. She was seriously injured and died some time later.

On hearing the news, the chief mobilized a group of people armed with spears and machetes to eliminate Apolo. Apolo then retreated to his house. Believing that he himself was armed with a spear, no one dared pursue him into the house. Their actions were limited to piercing the walls with spears. Chief Tabaro's mother finally intervened, exclaiming: "If you kill this man Apolo, who is alone in his house, for no reason, you will be killed in your turn. Indeed, the people feared the intervention of the English in Uganda, who would come to remove Chief Tabaro from his royal throne. Some Christians encountered at Apolo's home were severely beaten. Others took refuge in Toro. Then, after Apolo had been removed from his house, it was burnt down.

As for Apolo, he was beaten and then transferred to Mitego to the home of Chief Baligyangira, fiancé of the late Malyamu Taguita, who was careful not to shed the blood of this man of God. He resolved to transfer him to Toro (Uganda), to the home of an English officer, Captain Sitwell, so that he himself could answer the murder charges brought against him.
Chief Tabaro refUsa to give a piece of his territory to the Christians to build a church. He gave the following order to the Christians: (12).

- You won't build churches here;
- No one is allowed to   visit one   another .
  defeated ;
- You must not give food to catechists. Let them die or they will
  go elsewhere.

3.2 **Apolo Kivebulaya, his imprisonment and first vision**

When Apolo arrived in Uganda in 1898, he was put in prison at Fort Gerry to await trial. There, he had a greatly encouraging dream, which he later recounted (13):

Christ appeared to me in the dream during the night when I was wondering whether I should endure being tied up and pushed around with spears, and seeing my house burnt down, being beaten up every day, inveighed against and looked at with evil eyes. These were the things that tempted me to flee the Congo. While I was thinking about these things, I saw Jesus Christ shining like the sun and he said to me: "*Take courage, I am with you*". I replied, "*Who is he who speaks to me?* He answered for the second time, saying: "*I am Jesus Christ. Preach to my people. Do not be afraid*" (14).

And Apolo adds, "Since that year(1898), when I preached to people, they quickly abandoned their customs and repented."

4. Time to prepare at the ministry
4.1 The Baptism and Conversion of Chief Tabaro by Apolo Kivebulaya

Apolo Kivebulaya's succession of hardships did not prevent him from continuing his work in the mission field. As soon as he was released, and with the encouragement he had received during the dream in prison, he hurried back to Mboga on April 4, 1898, to continue the work he had already begun. Once again he faced much opposition and mistreatment, but he was patient and persevered in his faith. This was the beginning of his fruitful ministry among the natives. He succeeded in extending evangelization to other surrounding tribes.

Apolo succeeded in converting to Christianity the Tabaro chief whom no one believed could ever accept this religion, for he had at one time denied the existence of God and hated Apolo with all his heart, following the successive misfortunes which befell his locality in 1898 and which we have described in points 3.1 [1er period of 1er epoch] of this Book. And when Apolo asked Chief Tabaro for his sacred drum called *Rusuma* to use in church to keep the faithful from praying. When Chief Tabaro agreed to this, it was a great surprise for the pagans, and a great victory for the Gospel and for Apolo, for this drum was for the people, the symbol of the spirit of the tribe(. The chief began to support Apolo in his ministry, for which he was totally devoted. On November 28, 1898, Bishop Alfred Tucker made his first pastoral visit to Mboga. On this occasion, thirteen more people were baptized and the other seven first baptized were confirmed. The Christian community of Mboga was thus growing little by little.

4.2 Apolo Kivebulaya's ordination to the diaconate and priesthood

On December 21, 1900, Apolo Kivebulaya was ordained deacon in Kabarole in the kingdom of Toro. His ordination to the priesthood took place in June 1903 in Kampala. After his ordination, Apolo spent several years in Uganda, working for the Anglican Church in Toro and Mboga. From 1900 to 1915, Apolo served in various locations in Uganda (Toro, ...) while at the same time looking after the church in Mboga.

In 1916, Apolo returned to Mboga for good. He first set about strengthening the Christian community, then moved on to building churches (in pisé) in Mboga and surrounding villages.

Apolo church in Mboga

On November 5, 1917, Apolo went to Irumu, capital of the Ituri District, to seek authorization for the Anglican Church to operate officially on Congolese soil. This authorization was granted without any problem. From then on, he could continue his missionary activities in Mboga without fear, since until then he had seemed to be operating underground.

On October 3, 1919, Apolo built the first elementary school in Mboga. Following the reconstruction of the Mboga church and school, parents began bringing their children to learn to read and write. Within a few months, the Apolo residence was full of boys and girls. This was the beginning of the catechist training school.

On April 18, 1921, the District Commissioner arrived in Mboga to visit the school. He was very appreciative of the school and gave it many donations of benches, paper, chalk, etc. for its operation.

In the meantime, the evangelization effort concentrated in and around Mboga had made this a viable site. Mboga was already taking on the appearance of a missionary center for training and sending out catechists. Until then, Apolo had concentrated on evangelizing the savannah dwellers. Now he had to extend his work to the forest peoples to the south-east of Mboga.

4.3 Evangelization among forest dwellers

Apolo Kivebulaya, Apostle of the Pygmies

In Mboga, Apolo considered 1921 to be the year of the Gospel, with a great spiritual harvest. Ibrahimu Katalibara recounts how Apolo courageously asked the Tabaro chief for his sacred *"Rusama"* drum, to be used for calling Christians at worship time. For the people, this drum was the symbol of the tribe's spirit. It was kept in a secret place where a woman took care of it. This symbol of power was worshipped like a god, with its own shrine, priest and sacrificer. It was carried before the chief for traditional ceremonies, but once used for other purposes, it lost its power. This gesture on the part of the chief was therefore a source of great astonishment to the pagans (15).

Apolo recounts how God had encouraged him to go preaching in the forest: "As late as 1921, Christ appeared to me in the form of a man standing at my side. It was as if I saw a man who was my brother. He said to me: *'Go and preach in the forest because I am with you'*. I responded by asking, *"Who is this who speaks to me?"* He replied, *"I am what I am, this is my name"*. When I awoke, I set about the evangelical expedition" (16). The year 1921 thus marked the beginning of the evangelization of the forest peoples: the Balese, Nyali and Nande.

On the subject of Apolo Kivebulaya's pastoral voyages, it's worth noting that he kept a good logbook, as a good ship's captain usually does. On April 21, 1921, Apolo brought evangelists to the Walese of Kamenga village and Mount Hoyo... He continued his work in Banyanjao and Tchabi. When he arrived at the Sulemani chief's home in Kainama (in today's North Kivu province), he visited the evangelists he had sent earlier.

In 1921, Apolo built churches in Musango, Bundingiri and Mugenyi, among the Balese. In 1924, Apolo visited the churches of Bukima, Tchabi, Bundingiri and Kainama. A little later, he also built a church for the Pygmies in the forest.

April 11, 1924 marked the start of evangelization in Kamatsi (Bukiringi), among the Walendu Bindi. The chief of this Ituri tribe and his people had received the Good News without resistance, so Apolo left an evangelist to further strengthen them.

On September 8, 1924, Apolo continued to evangelize the Pygmies, leaving them an evangelist after spending a few days among them.

On September 14, 1925, Apolo went to Bwakadi. The Christians asked him for evangelists, but Apolo ran out of God's servants to give them.

In the end, the Gospel was preached to the Pygmies (Bambuti), a forest people who were often despised by the Banyamboga, because of their short stature (generally 1 m 40-45 cm) and their lifestyle, considered primitive and nomadic, living by hunting and gathering. But Apolo had made friends with them. He could eat their food and spend the night in their hut (17). In this way, he won their trust and their hearts for the cause of the Gospel.

From then on, the number of baptisms increased among both forest and savannah peoples. Chapels were built in all the regions surrounding Boga, and catechists were installed to provide spiritual guidance.

Many Pygmies were already baptized in the Mboga Church. But the first Pygmy baptism was performed by Apolo himself in 1932. It was his last visit to the forest. Nasani, one of Apolo's catechists, describes the baptism session as follows: "Apolo baptized two groups of Pygmies. These two groups had settled near Makanga, and he had taken great pains to teach them. When he baptized these groups, in one of them Apolo named all the men Abraham and all the women Sarah! In the other group, he named all the men Matthew and the women Mary" (18).

Apolo had not considered the difficulty of identification that these new imported names would probably cause these groups of Pygmies when naming or addressing each other. This practice was common in the churches of colonial times, which considered African surnames as belonging to the reign of the devil, to be replaced by biblical names after baptism.

In view of his great evangelical work among the Pygmy peoples, Apolo Kivebulaya was later nicknamed *"Apostle of the Pygmies"*.

4.4 Liturgy in converted territories

The other tribes joined the Anglican Church just as pagans joined Judaism through circumcision, or barbarians joined Hellenism by learning Greek wisdom.

In the Anglican Church, the catechism and the *Book of Common Prayer* in Kihema (Lunyoro) were imposed on all tribes indiscriminately, forcing them to learn Kihema in order to be baptized. Thus, conveyed by a foreign language, the Gospel seemed to be the prerogative of the Banyamboga people, the only ones who mastered the Kihema language. For the Lord's Supper, Apolo had taught the women to make bread as they did in their homes over the fire, and he himself made communion wine from banana juice when the stock of wine received from Toro was exhausted (19).

The imposition of the Lunyoro language was evident even in the administration of the Anglican Church, giving the impression of a cultural colonization of blacks by blacks. The Banyamboga thus had the lion's share of power in this Church, as they held local decision-making power over everything, to such an extent that the other tribes went so far as to refer to the Anglican Church as the "Church of the Bahema" (Kanisa la Bahema) and considered themselves dependent on them.

As for worship, it was conducted in the Kinyoro language even among other tribes, although most people understood little of it. *The* Kinyoro *Book of Common Prayer* was not translated into Swahili, or at least excerpts of it, until 1973, to give other tribes access to the liturgy.

Returning to the idea that for Anglicans, liturgy expresses faith, we understand that from 1896 to 1973, the tribes, for whom Kinyoro was not their mother tongue, worshipped without understanding exactly who and why they were worshipping (this situation was not so different from the pre-Vatican II Catholic Latin Mass). This had been a hindrance to the Evangelization of the Congo by the Anglicans (20). This is one of the reasons why the Anglican Church remained confined to a small corner of Ituri for so long. For eighty years, the Church has been self-marginalized, spreading out over a radius of just 80 km^2 , in a vast Congo that measures 2,345,409 km2 in area.

5. The organization of the Mboga mission station and Apolo's elevation to the rank of Canon

5.1 Mboga mission station

Apolo's working method, like that of all missionaries of the time, was to create mission stations on the mission fields. This was done through contacts that led to the creation of the first basic community made up of the first Christians in the area. This station was commonly known as a "*Mission*". The mission included the church building, the pastor's house and the houses of his catechists. Later, schools and teachers' houses were built. Some Christians were also allowed to live in the mission compound. This station was also intended to remove neophytes from their traditional environment, which was considered to be under the power of Satan.

It was therefore necessary to save souls from the harmful powers of ancestral tradition by protecting them on the mission field. Traditional songs and dances, alcoholic beverages and anything else customary were forbidden on the mission station. In the case of Mboga, as there was no boarding school, the neophytes were housed with families at the mission. This was also a way of teaching them the Hema language and culture.

Apolo's achievements were, all in all, very appreciable for a man of his standing, and no one doubts that his ministry was led by the Holy Spirit.

5.2 Apolo Kivebulaya, to the rank of canon

In recognition of his works to the glory of God, Apolo Kivebulaya was appointed and elevated to the rank of Canon of Namirembe Cathedral (Kampala), by letter of April 22, 1922 from Bishop J.J. Willis of the Church of Uganda (21).

The letter of appointment reads as follows.

Bishop's House

Kampala, Uganda

22 April 1922

To my brother,

I am very pleased to write to inform you that I have chosen you to be the Canon in the Church of Uganda with Rev. Mudeka. I have chosen you because of your spirit of patience and perseverance in the Church of Toro and Congo over all these years, and especially because of your endurance in suffering and persecution in the name of Our Lord, and for bringing this name to the pagans. For this reason, I consider you worthy of this honor. May God the Father increase in you the power and strength of the Holy Spirit, so that he may fulfill with joy and satisfaction your pilgrimage and the work for which he has called you.

Sincere greetings to all the Christians of Mboga.

I'm your brother who loves you.

J. J. Willis.

And in 1927, Canon Apolo Kivebulaya was elected Vice-President of the Church Missionary Society, and in June of the same year took part in the C.M.S. jubilee celebrations in Kampala (22).

5.3 Other Apolo activities to support the Church

Apolo Kivebulaya's work was not limited solely to proclaiming the Gospel. In the course of his ministry, he had touched on various aspects of life for the harmonious development of the community in whose midst he worked. He showed the faithful the importance of working in the fields, himself being an example in this field. He taught people how to reforest and plant eucalyptus trees to build proper, clean homes. Apolo insisted on cleanliness both inside and outside the house, cleanliness of clothes, cleanliness of the church, cleanliness of the body in general, and so on. He also taught them to read and write, so that they would be able to read the Word of God for themselves, and showed them the need for *stewardship* (tithes, offerings and the like).

We reported that in 1919 Apolo had begun building an elementary school in Mboga. This school became the nucleus around which several other schools were built. These schools were later recognized by the Belgian colonial state, whose emissaries visited the Mboga school in 1921. They did not hesitate to express their astonishment at the work carried out by a black missionary in this region. Of all the Protestant schools at the time, the Anglican school was the first to receive subsidies, at least in terms of benches, paper and chalk, from the Belgian colony, which had previously been concerned only with Catholic schools. It wasn't until 1948 that the Belgian colony began granting subsidies to Protestant schools.

Apolo had also set up a sort of outpatient dispensary in Mboga, which was occasionally visited by doctors from Uganda, and with whom he was sometimes accompanied on his pastoral visits.

Let's come back to teaching and its organization within the Anglican school. Generally speaking, during the colonial era, Anglican education, like all Protestant education, was primarily aimed at teaching baptismal candidates the rudiments of the alphabet, so that they could read the Holy Bible for themselves. Catechists were also selected from this group. So there were Christians who could only read their Bible, but who couldn't write at all.

Historically, Protestant schools were generally of a very low standard. Only Catholic schools, well-structured and supported by the Belgian state, provided training for the public administration and for their parishes.

The training given by Apolo and his successors in the Anglican Church in the Congo falls into the category of these literacy schools. Here's one of Anne Luck's descriptions of these schools: "The catechist who taught in the village was practically indistinguishable from the people he taught; he followed their habits without respecting the timetable. Sometimes he beat the drum in time (to invite people in), and sometimes he was late; one day he was working, another day he was absent. Children came in and out of the classroom, goats came in and ate the pieces of paper taped to the wall for reading. Teaching was jumbled and slow, but he (the teacher) still did a great job" (23).

We know that principals and teachers were provided by the Church of Uganda, an English-dominated colony, while the Congo Belge was a French-dominated colony. As a result, the people who studied there knew neither English nor French.

As for the training of God's servants, it should be noted that pastors went to Bible schools in Uganda. There, they received basic training in Swahili and Kinyoro. In the Congo, however, French, considered the language of the colonial administration and of esteem, was gaining ground. These pastors didn't even have access to specialized English-language Bible schools, either in Uganda or overseas. On the lay teaching side, the first instructors were Ugandans. They were gradually replaced by Congolese auxiliaries (with very modest training).

To enter the ministry, good conduct and humility were what counted, not intellectual training. Anne Luck describes Bishop Alfred Tucker's policy of religious formation in these terms: "It was Bishop Tucker's policy, in the early days of the mission, to ordain to the ministry men who had given evidence of Christian character and proof of leadership, though their intellectual achievement was less. This was the only means by which it was possible to make the sacraments available to many of the people who flocked to the Church" (24).

Apolo was one of these. He had never had the opportunity to study theology in the ordinary sense of the word, but his devotion, the holiness of his life, his understanding of people and his passion for mission, made him a man of extraordinary spiritual strength in the diocese (25).

This was understandable at a time when people's level of knowledge was very low and the policy of mass baptism was in full swing. Unfortunately, however, the policy of low education levels among church ministers remained the golden rule in the Anglican Church of the Congo from 1896 to 1980. This situation was denounced by Bishop Fidèle B. Dirokpa, Bishop of Bukavu at the time, in his inaugural address to the first diocesan synod held in Bukavu from January 6 to 13, 1983, in the following terms: "The Anglican Church of the Congo will soon be celebrating the centenary of its entry into the Congo, but it has no ministers trained to doctorate, master's or bachelor's level, not even to six-year secondary level, whereas in Uganda, the Church abounds with ministers of all these levels" (26).

We believe that the Church of Congo was disadvantaged by its French-speaking position, which meant that the C.M.S., with its strong roots in Uganda, was neglected. Then formation, even at the lowest level, was very slow and, when Apolo died after 37 years of ministry in the Congo, there were still no Congolese priests.

5.4 The Anglican Church in Ruanda-Urundi

Ruanda-Urundi, with which the Congo forms part of the Church of Uganda (along with the Anglican Church of the Congo), was evangelized by the Anglican Church from Uganda 29 years after the Congo.

In fact, the Anglican Church arrived in Rwanda in 1925 from Uganda via British missionaries. They belonged to the CMS/England Missionary Society through its branch called "Ruanda-Mission". The best-known missionaries in this group were Captain Geoffrey Holmes and Reverend Halord Guillebaud. Anglicanism's first point of entry into Rwanda was Gahini.

On June 6, 1966, Rwanda's first diocese, that of Kigali, was inaugurated with its first Bishop Mgr Adonia Sebununguri. In 1975, this diocese split in two, giving rise to the Diocese of Butare, with the consecration of Bishop Justin Ndandali on November 19, 1975.

Burundi was evangelized by the Anglican Church of Uganda on January 1er 1935 by two white missionaries from CMS/England accompanied by a Ugandan evangelist.
The Anglican Church's first point of entry in Burundi was BUHIGA, where Dr Len Sharpen had already been working in the hospital since 1930. He was then joined in 1935 by Algemon Stanley Smith, Dr Bill Church and Kosiya Shalita, a Ugandan.

The first Anglican diocese in Burundi is BUYE, with Bishop Jean Nkunzumwami, and the 2nd^{e} is Bjumbura, with Bishop Samuel Sindamuka.

5.5 The last days of Apolo Kivebulaya

Towards the end of 1932, Apolo felt weakened by hard work, but continued his pastoral activities normally until February 1933. Feeling increasingly weak, he left Mboga on February 24, 1933 for Mengo hospital in Kampala.

Dr. Sir Albert Cook examined him and told him that his heart was tired. He prescribed three months' rest, but feeling that his time to die was at hand, Apolo asked to be transported to Mboga, to die among the people he loved dearly and who also loved him; this was done. As soon as he arrived in Mboga, his situation worsened.

Reverend Russell and his wife were sent from Uganda to assist him in his final moments. It is with emotion that we listen to Apolo Kivebulaya's last interview on his sickbed, as rendered by this delegation: "Concerning the work on the mission field, I asked him who would continue this work. He replied: 'Thomasi Ndahura, Nasani Kabarole, Yosia Kaburwa, YusufU Limenya, they will be able to help the Mboga Church, I have trained them well. I asked him if he had any money in the bank. And he replied: 'I don't even have a shilling in the bank. I asked him if he had any debts, and he replied: 'There are no debts, except for a few shillings belonging to Thomasi Ndahura, which he had entrusted to me to place in the fund intended to pay the forest catechists, 250 shillings. Sell my table and chairs and teapot and so on to repay these shillings". He then added that he had 2 cows in Butiti. Leave them," said Apolo, "for the Mboga church. (27). He had nothing in the true sense of the word.

After 38 years of remarkable missionary work in Uganda and Congo, Apolo Kivebulaya died on May 30, 1933 at 2:45 pm, in Mboga (28). He was buried on May 31, 1933 in the garden of the Mboga parish church, in the presence of numerous Christians and other personalities, including the chief of the Mboga locality and even the white Belgian colonial authorities. This testified to the esteem in which they held Apolo Kivebulaya, because of the remarkable evangelization and instruction work he had carried out on the mission field in this region.

Before his death, Apolo had said: "Let me go and meet those of my children who have gone before me to heaven, so that I may be with my Lord whom I have served from my youth to my old age". His request then consisted of two things: firstly, he forbade weeping and mourning at his death, and secondly, he had wished to be buried with his head turned towards the forest [West]"(29) and his feet towards the East. This was contrary to Banyamboga custom, which requires a man to be buried with his head turned towards his home. With this gesture, Apolo wanted to signify that his spirit was still on the move to evangelize the peoples of the forest, i.e. all the way to the end of the Congo, as the equatorial forest crosses this great country from east to west, all the way to the Atlantic Ocean.

At the time of his death, his field of evangelization included Irumu Territory in Province Orientale and the town of Kainama, on the northern border of Kivu Province. In the meantime, he had already trained 75 native catechists, but there were as yet no ordained ministers.

5.6 Apolo Kivebulaya, a model servant of God

In more ways than one, Apolo Kivebulaya's life and work are an example to be followed by God's ministers, constantly driven by the goals of missionary success in the field of evangelization.

5.6.1. A modest servant

Behind the desire to deprive ministers of religion of a respectable standard there may have been other aims. We're thinking, for example, of the Belgian colonial system based on paternalism, which translated into the maxim: "No elites, no trouble". It was necessary to train servants who would pay slavish allegiance to their bosses in the Church hierarchy or to financial backers. Servants were needed who knew nothing of the secular sciences; this obliged them not to abandon the ministry, since they could not have the ambition or ability to do anything else in society because of their knowledge limited only to the rudiments of the Bible. Finally, servants were needed who could be used as free labor.

These words from Mgr Mbona Kolini, then Bishop of Katanga, sum up the situation experienced by the Church's ministers and their flock:

"I know people who haven't eaten for three or four days but I still see them singing and dancing in Church. Why is that? I can only attribute it to the work of the Holy Spirit. Day by day, people are brought to understand that their only security is in the Lord" (30).

5.6.2. Apolo Kivebulaya, a model of exceptional dedication

Since his conversion to Christianity, Apolo had devoted his entire life to spreading the Gospel. He was a patient and persevering man, humble and devoted, a man of prayer and faithful, endowed with the gift of healing. Above all, he was a man of great faith and zeal for the Lord's service. The Lord had equipped him as he had so many other of his seasoned servants, whom we meet in the Bible and in Church history.

Like the Apostle Paul, Apolo had first taken part in the martyrdom of Christians. As a new convert, he had more zeal for the Gospel than long-standing Christians. He had been unjustly slandered, beaten several times, expelled and imprisoned. He did manual labor to support himself without being a burden on others. He travelled great distances across the savannah and the forest with the sole aim of bringing the Gospel to the pagans. Despite his low intellectual level, he was able to introduce Anglicanism to the Congo. He did not hesitate to confront peoples and customs unknown in Congo and Uganda. His ministry, which began with difficulties, would later prove fruitful.

All in all, Apolo had the scope to continue his work in the Congo. It's up to his followers in God's work to imitate his example and spread Anglicanism throughout the Congo and beyond.

5.6.3. Apolo Kivebulaya, an African Saint

Apolo Kivebulaya is honored as a Saint in the Anglican Church of Congo and Uganda, as well as throughout East Africa. His effigy is in the stained glass window of All Saints Cathedral in Nairobi, Kenya. Anne Luck writes: "Apolo Kivebulaya fat was a man of apostolic quality. Even if other Christians cannot be put on the same footing as the Apostles of Jesus who testified to the resurrection of their Master, Apolo was, in the truest sense, the Apostle of the Church of Mboga, and his life bore witness to the reality of the living Christ" (31).

This text, written on the left cover on the inside page of Anne Luck's book "African Saint", about Apolo Kivebulaya, further testified to his life of holiness:

"Apolo of Uganda and Congo, who died in 1933, would probably have to be chosen, if the Anglican Communion were to recognize anyone from East Africa, as a saint. Through many circumstances, he was, by the same title, the Anglican Saint Francis or the Curé d'Ars, living very close to the Equator. *It was as if I was seeing a man who was my friend,* as he said of one of his visions of Christ. His humble joy drew his own people to Uganda, and his courage brought the Gospel to the Pygmies of the equatorial forest. His story is important for the universal Church, because in our world, an authentically African Christianity has been born, and the universal Church should be aware of Africans of Apolo's stature".

Apolo and his followers spread the Gospel and maintained the Anglican presence in the Congo until it was officially recognized as a diocese in 1972, after three quarters of a century (76 years) of hard work in the faith.

5.6.4. **Apolo Kivebulaya, a monument of the Anglican Church of Congo**

Apolo remains a monument in the history of the Anglican Church in Congo and Uganda, but the influence of Mboga and the mythical cult of Apolo is gradually waning with the creation of other dioceses in Congo.

Certainly, they recognize in him the merits of holiness of life and zeal for the Gospel of Jesus Christ, as well as the model of love for God's people. As a result, they find his ministry exemplary, inspiring and encouraging, and would like to imitate him as a faithful servant of God, rather than make of him a mythical figure, to the point of neglecting the essentials of the faith.

PARTIAL CONCLUSION

The first period, from 1896 to 1933, was one of preparing the field and sowing the seeds of the Good News. Apolo Kivebulaya remains the figurehead of this period. This was the period when Anglican missionaries from Uganda planted good seed in Congolese soil.

These seeds grew despite the brambles and thorns that sought to choke them, and bore fruit that the Anglican Church is proud of today. Like a mustard seed, too small, weak and invisible to the naked eye, set in the sometimes fierce soil, the Anglican Church of Congo is proud to see itself become a great tree despite all the weaknesses that still characterize it. The Church has stood firm through difficult days because the Holy Spirit was present.

These men, with little education and no material means whatsoever, on the one hand, and working in an officially Catholic territory whose government was hostile to other religious denominations, on the other, maintained the presence of the Anglican faith in the Congo. However, it should be noted that the shortcomings of the beginning are still felt today in certain sectors of Church activity, both in the field of management training and in those of the socio-economic life of God's servants, evangelization, liturgy, and so on. In the previous part of this first chapter, we highlighted the role played by Apolo and his ministry, and demonstrated the strengths and weaknesses of the missionary works of this period. We now turn to the transition after Apolo's death.

NOTES

Period A of the Ugandan Missionaries.

(1) Anne Luck, "*African Saint, the story of Apolo Kivebulaya*", Great Britain, SCM Press Ltd, 1963, p. 68.

[This book was used extensively in the 1st chapter because of its wealth of information on the life and works of Apolo Kivebulaya].

(2) Ibid. p.24

(3) Ibid. p.61

(4) Ibid. p.62

(5) Ibid. p.116

(6) Ibid. 123

(7) Ibid, p.68

(8) Ibid. p.69

(9) Ibid. p.69

(10)   Ibid. p.72

(11)   Ibid. p.72

(12)   Ibid. p.74

(13)   Ibid. p.76

(14)   Ibid. p.77

(15)   Ibid.p.79

(16)   .ibid. p. 123

(17)   Ibid. p. 124

(18)   Ibid. p. 145

(19)   Ibid. p. 142

(20)   Isingoma Kahwa: *Où va l'EAZ*? 1992, unpublished.

(21)   Anne Luck, op.cit. p.125

(22)   Ibid. 138

(23)   ANGLICAN CHURCH OF ZAIRE: "Kwa Imani Apolo, Gateshead (Great Britain), Paradigm Print, 1986, p.20

(24)   Ibid.p.101

(25)   Ibid.p.102

(26)   The first Bukavu diocesan synod, January 6-13, 1983,

(27)   Ibid,p.147

(28)   Ibid.p.148

(29)   Ibid.p.147

(30)   Mgr Mbona Kolini, in *Centenary of the Anglican Church in Zaire,* 1996, p.25.
(31)   Anne Luc, op.cit. p.12

Part 2
SECOND PERIOD OF THE MISSIONARY ERA
Chapter 2
B. EXPATRIATE MISSIONARIES AND THE CONSOLIDATION OF THE WORK OF APOLO KIVEBULAYA (1933-1960)

This second stage in the evolution of the Anglican Church of the Congo covers the period from 1933, the death of Apolo Kivebulaya, to 1960, the year of Congo's independence, which coincided with the desire for Africanization of the leadership in all areas.

Apolo's death came as a great shock to the Mboga Anglican Church. It had just lost in his person a leader and a pastor who had won the trust of the faithful through his great love for his flock, a love without discrimination of gender or tribe and totally dedicated to the work of the Gospel. Apolo did not simply preach the Gospel, but his whole life was a living preaching of the demands of the Christian life, following the will of Christ. After him, qualified people were needed to take over the activities of this valiant man of God. The post-Apolo Kivebulaya period was marked by three important events: the arrival of white missionaries in Mboga, the promotion of pastoral ministry and teaching, and the independence of the Congo and freedom of worship.

1. European missionaries in Mboga: arrival and promotion policy

Before his death, and drawing on his experience in Uganda, where British missionaries had long been at work, Apolo had expressed a desire to welcome men of God from Europe into his community. The reason for this was that, until then, no Congolese had been trained for the diaconate or the priesthood. What's more, the catechists present in the region had only attended the literacy school to read the Bible, of which they had received the rudiments. Anne Luck notes: "Apolo urged CMS to send a European missionary to take over the expanding work in Mboga. Although he hoped that the catechists he had appointed would continue to be trained for ordination, for he himself knew the need for a well-trained and educated missionary to consolidate the work he had begun as a pioneer" (1).

Apolo Kivebulaya's wish had been heard. In June 1933, Albert Lloyd, a retired missionary from Uganda, was sent to Mboga. He was followed, in February 1934, by a young missionary, Charles A. Rendle. But before they arrived, another Ugandan missionary, Anania Binaisha, had already been sent to Mboga to take temporary charge of the Church.

In 1935, the English missionary Reverend R.C. Pelin arrived in Mboga. He was to take charge of the church and the training of catechists. As a lay missionary, Rendle was in charge of teaching (2) In 1950, the Reverend Philip Ridsdale arrived in Mboga. He took over responsibility for teaching, while also building schools and churches. He later became the first bishop of the Anglican Church of Congo in 1972.

The permanent presence of European missionaries was necessary in the Belgian colony of Congo, where the Belgian colonizer, laden with negative prejudices about the black man and his cultures, showed contempt for the latter. Indeed, the Belgian government refused to recognize the concession of the Mboga mission because of the lack of resident white missionaries, whom it considered valid interlocutors, despite the rivalries that characterized missionary work in the field of evangelization in the Belgian Congo, notably between the Catholic Church and other religious denominations.

European missionaries were entrusted with ministry and teaching in their own communities. To do this, foreign missionaries first had to pass through the Ecole Coloniale in Antwerp, Belgium, to receive instructions on how to treat the black man and to learn French, which was the official language of the colony.

It's a fact that, despite the good will of these European missionaries, they couldn't make spectacular progress like the Catholic Church, which had a monopoly on the mission to Christianize and civilize the Congolese.

The text of the Convention of May 26, 1906 between Leopold II, King of the Belgians and the Holy Apostolic See, commented on by Crawford Young, put forward the principle that would remain in force until 1960:

"The missionary effort was to be mainly of Belgian origin (...). The Concordat of 1960 established a framework for cooperation between the missions and the administration. The State not only subsidized Catholic mission schools, but also contributed to the upkeep of missionaries. Another very important aid was the official granting of 200 hectares of land to any mission established in the Congo, which could use it both for commercial purposes and to meet its own needs" (3).

It's clear that the Catholic missions have made great strides in development in the Congo with the support of the Belgian government.

The Anglican community in the Congo greatly appreciates the evangelizing work of Anglican missionaries and remains grateful to them. However, we do not believe that the Belgian government prohibited other religious denominations from developing the areas where their missions were located. The proof is that other denominations, such as the Presbyterians, Baptists, Methodists, Mennonites, etc., although left to their own devices, had nevertheless developed their missions and made appreciable progress in the field of instruction for their Christians.

The C.M.S. policy was to let the natives find/discover their own needs and then allow the Missionary Society to get involved. This could be a good way of letting people reflect on their own situation, and since it's their wish, they'd be more likely to get involved. However, how could the Congolese in the bush be aware of the new technology that the European missionary was the only one to offer them?

This policy, we believe, caused serious delays in many areas of the development of the Anglican Church of the Congo. If we compare, even today, the missionary station of Mboga with the other missionary stations created in the   former British colonies,   we wonder whether the   expatriate   missionaries have
actually lived in Mboga. In the case of Bishop Philip Ridsdale, the first bishop of the Mboga diocese, he lived in a straw-roofed house until his retirement in 1980.

Let's face it, the missionaries did what they could in a totally Catholic colony, and no one should hold that against them. We can, however, point out that this situation was no hindrance to the Gospel, which was preached by courageous evangelists of good faith, patient and loving their Lord, under the inspiration of the Holy Spirit.

The Anglican Church of the Congo lacks the material resources and competent personnel to carry out consistent work: theological discussions on African and other religions, inculturation in the fields of evangelization, catechesis, liturgy, etc. It is high time to rectify this situation by giving some priority to training religious leaders and Christians, without neglecting other development projects. It's high time to put things right by giving priority to the training of religious leaders and Christians, without neglecting other development projects.

2. Promotion in ministry and teaching

2.1. The first ordination of Congolese to the diaconate and priesthood

The first Congolese to be elevated to the diaconate were Nasani Kabarole and Yusufu Limenya. They were ordained deacons in 1937, then priests in 1940. The single parish of Boga, created by Apolo Kivebulaya in 1897, had to wait 41 years before being split into two: Boga and Kainama. The Reverend Nassani Kabarole remained   incumbent of the Boga parish   ,
             by virtue of the parish'   s   population of
Mboga, Walendu/Bindi and Walese regions, while Reverend YusufU Limenya was in charge of the Kainama parish. He was responsible for the Nyali, Talinga, Nande and Pygmy areas in the forest. After this event, a number of God's servants were sent to Bible schools in Uganda. Indeed, the Reverends Nasani Kabarole and Limenya Yusufu had undergone accelerated theological training at Uganda's Mukono College. As the number of Congolese priests in the mission field increased, more parishes and chapels were opened to strengthen evangelization.

Shortly before the Congo gained independence, the Anglican Church experienced a certain growth, with new ordinations to the ministry and the opening of new parishes as the number of clergy increased, notably that of Bukiringi among the Walendu/Bindi, created in 1946; that of Bundingiri among the Walese, created in 1947; that of Ofayi, founded in 1955, and that of Kamango, among the Watalinga and Amba, which came into being in 1956.

In 1947, Bishop Alberi Balya was consecrated. He was the first African bishop in East Africa. The Anglican station of Mboga was included in his jurisdiction.

Finally, between 1930 and 1960, many missionaries from Uganda made pastoral visits to Boga. Among them were bishops who came to confirm the faithful.

2.2.   Approval of Anglican schools by the Belgian colonial government

As far as education was concerned, missionary Rendle had made a considerable effort to supervise the schools Apolo had left behind. However, these followed the Ugandan curriculum. Even the teachers came from Uganda.

In 1948, the Mboga elementary school was approved by the provincial inspector of elementary school, enabling it to receive regular subsidies from the colonial government, like other Protestant schools.

In 1951, the schools in Mboga, Bukiringi and Bundingiri were visited by a Belgian education inspector. On this occasion, most of the classes were subsidized. Mr Rendle, who had returned from Belgium for his colonial course, was recognized as Director and Missionary Inspector of the elementary school.

It should be pointed out that, at that time, most of these schools were still at primary or lower secondary level. The first Ugandan monitors were gradually replaced by Congolese auxiliaries (of modest training), still under the direction of Mr Rendle.

3. The lunyoro liturgy

During this period of European missionaries, the liturgy continued to be celebrated in Lunyoro. All liturgical documents were in Lunyoro: the Bible, the Book of Common Prayer, the songbook, etc. The surrounding population was still obliged to learn this new language, spoken in Uganda and by the Banyamboga. The surrounding population was still obliged to learn this new language, spoken in Uganda and by the Banyamboga, in order to attend catechism classes and participate in worship.

4. A local church

The Banyamboga considered the Anglican Church to be their private property. They were right to do so, for as Georges Titre Ande states: "The Church of England in the Congo was established mainly thanks to Chief Paulo Tabaro II (17ᵉ king of the Mboga dynasty), who went to see Chief Kasagama of Toro, Uganda, to bring this region under British jurisdiction. Contact with the teachings on the new faith enabled Tabaro to ask evangelists to come and spread these teachings in Mboga"(4).

Legitimate because: "*Cuius regio, illius religio*" or "*Like prince, like religion*", *as* the saying goes. It was thanks to Chief Paulo Tabaro II of the Banyamboga that the teachings of the new faith, the Anglican Church, were introduced to Mboga.

However, for a long period of 84 years (1896-1980), this Church remained under the administration and total control of the Church of Uganda, which was itself under the control of England. The fate of the Anglican Church of Congo was thus decided in Uganda, although from 1976 onwards, a French-speaking Council was created with a degree of autonomy for the Anglican Church of Burundi, Rwanda and Congo, which was part of the Ecclesiastical Province of Uganda. The synods that decided the fate of the Church were held in Uganda, without the Congolese being involved in any substantial way in the decisions. The central administration for all Church affairs was in Uganda. In this situation, the Banyamboga were better suited to represent the Church of the Congo, especially as they knew the Ugandan languages well.

5. The grain of Anglicanism in Masisi (North Kivu) by Rwandan immigrants (1936)

Rwandan immigrants were behind the establishment of Anglicanism in the Masisi territory as early as 1936. In 1950, however, the mission was abandoned due to political conflicts between the Belgians and the British.

A second stream of Anglicans came from Rwanda to settle in the Masisi territory in 1960. Unfortunately, in 1967, the Anglican Church closed its doors once again after the departure of two Ugandan evangelists: Canon Mukasa and Reverend Cibacibere.

6. The penetration of the Anglican Church in Elisabethville (Lubumbashi) from Northern Rhodesia (1950)

Anglicanism's presence in the former Katanga province dates back to the early 1950s, when the Anglican Church of Northern Rhodesia, now Zambia, sent priests to the Belgian Congo border to serve immigrant workers in the Copperbelt.

In 1954, the activities of the Anglican Church of Congo began under the episcopate of Bishop Owen of the Diocese of Northern Zambia, working under the aegis of the missionaries of the United Society for Propagating the Gospel (USPG) of England.

The Anglican Church of Elisabethville (Lubumbashi) began with a small group of immigrant Bemba workers in this locality. These Zambian Anglicans were from the High Church (Anglo-Catholic) tradition, and a priest came from Zambia once a month to celebrate mass. They occupied a small building abandoned by the German Reformed Church. This church was confined solely to the Bemba tribe and the British colonists working for the Union Minière du Haut Katanga. It did not expand, either in the town of Elisabethville or in other parts of Katanga province. The church was run by Sébastien Chungupengu, the very first catechist, who ministered from 1950 until political difficulties caused membership to dwindle after Congo's independence. In 1970, Pascal Chamfya voluntarily took charge of the Church as a catechist, without payment of any kind. He was ordained a priest on the arrival of Bishop Mbona Kolini Emmanuel, then Assistant Bishop of the Diocese of Bukavu.

7. The Anglican Church of Congo in the Protestant Council of Congo (CPC)

The Anglican Church of Congo, located in the Mboga area, far from other churches and major urban centers, left its isolation in 1956 to join the CONSEIL PROTESTANT DU CONGO (CPC).

Indeed, Protestant missionaries working on the mission field in the Belgian Congo had held an International Meeting in Edinburgh (Scotland) in 1910, with a view to forming a platform to defend the interests of Protestant churches in the Belgian Congo, where Protestantism was relegated to second place. [It was only after Congo's independence that Protestant churches invaded the major centers. The Anglican Church of Congo took a decade after independence to move from its Mboga base to the major centers].

Following the Edinburgh International Meeting, the "Conseil Protestante du Congo" was formed and approved by the Belgian government in 1924. It was authorized to operate officially, while defending the rights of Protestant missions in the Belgian Congo. Participants were mainly European missionaries. The Anglican Church of the Congo did not yet have valid representatives to take part in this organization. So, with the presence of European missionaries in Mboga, the Anglican Church of Congo joined this platform in 1956.

PARTIAL CONCLUSION

In Apolo's day, white missionaries visited the Mboga church, mainly to administer the sacraments, but they had never lived on Mboga soil. It was only after the death of this great man of God that expatriate missionaries from C.M.S./England came to reside on the evangelization field at Mboga. They took over from Apolo Kivebulaya.

The Church is now under the leadership of the C.M.S. missionaries, still under the ecclesiastical jurisdiction of Uganda.

The work of evangelization continued, as did the planting of new chapels and the emphasis on training for pastoral ministry. The first Congolese Anglican priests were ordained, and parishes were opened. Education and social work were also on the agenda.

Anglican elementary school were approved by the Belgian colonial government, which also granted them subsidies. The Anglican Church thus left its isolation and joined the platform: Conseil Protestant du Congo (CPC).

NOTES

Period B of expatriate missionaries

(1)   Anne Luck, "*African Saint, the story of Apolo Kivebulaya*", Great Britain, SCM Press Ltd, 1963, p. 149

(2)   Bezaleri Ndahura, *Implantation de l'Église anglicane au Zaïre, Mémoire de licence, Kinshasa, Faculté Protestante de Théologie, 1974, p. 84 (unpublished)*.

(3)   C. Young, *Introduction to Congolese politics, Kinshasa-Kisangani-Lubumbashi, Ed. Universitaires du Congo, 1968, p. 14.*

(4)   Georges Titre Ande, *L'Eglise anglicane du Congo: une province francophone,* in Anglicanism A Global Communion, by Andrew Wingate, Kevin Ward & Carrie Pemberton (Ed.) Nowbray, 1998, p.98.

Part 3

SECOND ERA
THE ANGLICAN CHURCH OF CONGO UNDER THE LEADERSHIP OF
CONGOLESE LEADERS (1960-2016)

Two important sections will be developed in this part of our study: the rise of the Anglican Church and its influence after the centenary of its establishment in the Congo.

Chapter 3

A. DEVELOPMENT OF THE ANGLICAN CHURCH OF CONGO: FROM INDEPENDENCE TO THE CENTENARY OF THE CHURCH'S ESTABLISHMENT (1960-1996)

1. Congo's independence and freedom of worship

1.1. Congo's independence

Following the Berlin Conference in 1885, which established an international settlement to put an end to rivalries between European powers in Africa and thereby ensure effective occupation of the dark continent, the lands under the direct ion of the Association Africaine pour le Congo (AIC) came under the authority of the Belgian King, Leopold II, who made it an independent state for his own benefit. In 1908, the Belgian parliament agreed to take over the Congo and make it a colony. The Congo Independent State then became the Belgian Congo until I960.

It should be noted that, after the First World War (1914-1918), Ruanda-Urundi, a German colony and an integral part of the Anglican Church of Uganda-as well as the Congo-became a territory under a mandate granted by the League of Nations (SDN) to Belgium. It should be noted that Belgium would later refer to the territory as Congo Belge and Ruanda-Urundi.

On June 30, 1960, the Belgian Congo gained independence and became the Republic of Congo. Its President was Joseph Kasavubu and its Prime Minister, Patrice Emery Lumumba. Ruanda-Urundi would remain a Belgian-ruled trust territory. It was not until July 1er 1962 that Rwanda and Burundi gained their independence, becoming two autonomous countries: the Republic of Rwanda (on 01/07/1962) and the Republic of Burundi (on 02/07/1962).

When the Congo gained independence, after eighty years of Belgian colonization, there was no serious preparation for the Congolese to take over the reins of the country in the political, administrative or church spheres. The Congolese were thus obliged to use their common sense in leadership positions. Nevertheless, significant progress was made in the exercise of religious ministry.

1.2. Freedom of worship

At independence, with the state declared secular, all Congolese were free to practice the religion of their choice. This marked the end of the monopoly of the Roman Catholic Church, which had been the state church during the colonial era. However, the influence of the Catholic Church, the sole provider of good schools and solid social structures, was to be felt for a long time to come in the administration and even in the social and political affairs of the independent Congo. In fact, most of the post-independence Catholic rulers did not hesitate to pursue religious and social discrimination in many cases.

However, in terms of law, Protestants and Catholics were on the same footing. They all received the same facilities from the State to better educate youth and exercise their apostolate.

In fact, following the recognition of freedom of worship for all at Congo's independence, certain religious movements that had resisted colonial oppression and achieved an appreciable level of organization, came out of hiding to engage in open proselytizing: Kimbanguism, Bapostolo, Vandism, Nsambi ka Yololo, Bundu Diakongo, Islam, etc. became, moreover, fully-fledged churches or government-recognized religions.

On the other hand, some nationals founded new ecclesial communities that were soon recognized by the state. All these communities confessed Christ and claimed to be orthodox Christians. At the same time, Protestant communities and Catholic missionary congregations that had never been active in the Congo also arrived. The country remained an open field for other foreign and national communities. All these communities settled down and devoted themselves to evangelization, education, medical work and development, alongside those who had been there since colonization. They raced against the clock in a spirit of competition, occupying every corner of the country. It was during this period that the Anglican Church left its home in Mboga to join other churches in the field of evangelization throughout the Congo. For the natives, freedom of worship meant that they could worship in the church of their choice. As a result, some even engaged in "spiritual prostitution", becoming members of several churches at the same time.

It's also worth noting the numerous dissidences among the various Protestant communities, mainly for tribal reasons, economic and financial interests, or the race for power. This often led to the creation of new communities with the same names, but without a visibly distinct doctrine.

2. Civil personality

When the Anglican Church was still in the hands of African missionaries and expatriates alike, its expansion was very slow.

When the country gained its independence, the Anglican Church of Congo, after 64 years of existence, had 6 parishes, 90 chapels and many elementary school. At that time, it was already present in three   administrative provinces of the Congo   :   the Province of Congo, the Province of Congo and the Province of Congo.

Orientale, Kivu and Katanga.

After the hasty departure of the missionaries following the unfortunate events of independence, the national members of the Anglican Church of Congo realized the need to extend their church to other provinces of the country.

At the same time, the legal representatives of the non-profit association *"Eglise Anglicane Congolaise"* applied to the Congolese government for civil status on May 17, 1960. This status was granted by Presidential Order of December 1ᵉʳ 1960, published in the *Moniteur Congolais*, n°1 of January 3 1961 (Official Journal of the Republic of Congo at the time). This ordinance marked the official recognition of the Congolese Anglican Church by the government, and authorized it to operate legally throughout the country.

Here is the text of the Ordinance granting civil personality to the association *"Eglise Anglicane Congolaise"*, while officially recognizing its leaders:

REPUBLIC OF CONGO

Ordinance granting civil status to the "Eglise Anglicane Congolaise" association.

The President of the Republic;

Considering the fundamental law of May 19, 1960, especially article 20;

In view of the constitutional decree-law of September 29, 1956;

In view of the decree of November 27, 1959 on non-profit associations;

Having regard to the request dated May 17, 1960 from the legal representatives of the "Eglise Anglicane Congolaise" association;

On the proposal of the General Commissioner for Justice;

Order:

Article 1.

Civil status is granted to the "Eglise Anglicane Congolaise" association, based in Mboga, Bunia Territory, Province Orientale, whose purpose is evangelism, teaching, and medical and social work among the population.

The association's legal representative is Mr Ndahura Bezaleri, schoolteacher, and its deputy legal representatives are Mr Byakisaka Festo, Pastor, and Mr Mwaka Isaka, Schoolteacher, all of whom live in Mboga.

Art icle 3.

The Commissioner General for Justice is responsible for the execution of this order.

Leopoldville, December 1ᵉʳ 1960.
J. KASA-VUBU
For the President of the Republic,
The General Commissioner for Justice
M. LIAHU.

The Congolese churches, which until then had been run by white missionaries, were gradually handed over to national leaders. The year 1960 marked a decisive step towards Congolese leadership of the Church. With the advent of independence, the missionaries were forced to hand over the leadership of the churches to the nationals. So, on December 1, 1960, when the Congolese Anglican Church obtained its civil personality, as mentioned in this Ordinance, it had its 1st officially recognized Congolese Legal Representative.

In 1961, Rev. Festo Byakisaka was appointed Dean of the Congolese Anglican Church by the Bishop of the Diocese of Ruwenzori. In this capacity, he replaced Rev. Walugyo, a Ugandan. In 1968, the Congolese Anglican Church was erected as an Archdeaconry, with its seat in Mboga. Rev. Festo Byakisaka became the first Archdeacon.

3. The handover with CMS or the official transfer of responsibilities to the Congolese

The Church Missionary Society (CMS), which had supported the Congolese Anglican Church from the outset, now saw the need to hand over the management of the Mboga Church to the Congolese leaders appointed by the Presidential Ordinance of December 1ᵉʳ 1960 and to others, at all levels and in all fields.

On January 30, 1967, CMS officially wrote a letter to the Bishop of the Diocese of Ruwenzori, transferring the authority and responsibility it held to the indigenous church of Mboga:

CHURCH MISSIONARY SOCIETY
Telephone: Kampala 64044
Telegram: 'Testimony, Kampala'
Office: Namirembe
P.O.Box 14051 Kampala, Uganda
January 30, 1967
To the Bishop of Ruwenzori
P. O. Box 37 Fort Portai
Concerns: CMS and Anglican Church of Congo, Mboga.
Dear Bishop,
I am writing to you regarding the relationship between CMS on the one hand, and EAC on the other. Since the Society has been unable to find a replacement for Mr. Rendle, and it would appear that there will be little hope of posting missionaries there in the future, I am sure that the responsibilities should be officially transferred to the Congolese Anglican Church (EAC).
I am therefore writing to you on behalf of the CMS to relinquish all responsibility formerly held by our missionary society for the finances and administration of the medical, educational and pastoral works carried out within the Mboga Church. I hereby authorize the transfer of authority and responsibility to the Anglican Church of Congo.
Sincerely yours,
Sé/NORMAN,
CMS Representative /Uganda (1)

4. Changing the church's name

The members of the EAC's executive board, having examined the initial name of their non-profit association (ASBL), decided to modify it and give it a more appropriate name. Instead of "Eglise Anglicane Congolaise", they opted for "*Eglise Anglicane du Congo*", which they felt was more expressive.

The Executive Council of the Anglican Church of Congo has decided to use the name "Anglican" and the preposition "du" instead of *au.* The idea is that it is not the Church of the English that is being transferred to the Congo, but rather a Congolese Church that shares the doctrine of the Church as interpreted by the Anglican Reformation (2).

Thus, on July 1er 1967, the majority of the EAC's full members sent a letter to the Ministry of Justice, requesting a modification to their Statutes of 1960, especially with regard to the article concerning the name of the Church. Their request was granted, and here is the text of the Ministerial Order.

DEMOCRATIC REPUBLIC OF CONGO

MINISTRY OF JUSTICE

31st DIRECTION

WORSHIP ADMINISTRATION AND ASSOCIATIONS

Ministerial Decree no. 108/68 of 10/07/68 approving the amendment to the articles of association of the non-profit association "Eglise Anglicane Congolaise".

The Minister of Justice;

In view of the decree-law of September 18, 1965, relating to non-profit associations, especially articles 12 and 13;

In view of the order of December 1er 1960, granting the non-profit association "Eglise anglicane congolaise" civil personality.

In view of the ministerial decree of January 11, 1967, approving the articles of association and the appointment of persons responsible for the administration or management of the above mentioned non-profit association;

In view of the decision dated July 1, 1967 by the majority of the full members of the same association;

ARRETE:

Sole article:

The decision taken on July 1er 1967 by the majority of the full members of the non-profit association "Eglise Anglicane Congolaise" is hereby approved, giving it the name *"Eglise Anglicane du Congo"*, in abbreviation: EAC.

Kinshasa, July 10, 1968,

Sé/ J. N'SINGA

Member of the MPR Political Bureau.

For certified copy,

Kinshasa, 20/07/1968

For the Director Head of Department,

The Deputy Director Head of Section,

Sé/B. BAKPABUA.-

5. The Anglican Church of Congo expands beyond Mboga

Before 1968, EAC had already been introduced in three provinces: Province Orientale, Kivu and Katanga.

The Anglican Church of the Congo underwent spectacular expansion as the indigenous population took over. It left the Mboga region to reach the cities, major towns and other administrative provinces of the Democratic Republic of Congo.

From 1968 onwards, the Anglican Church expanded into the town of Bunia in the north (120 km from Mboga) and into the Beni and Lubero Territories in the south (200 km from Mboga), in the

Kivu Province. From Bunia, it also reached Kisangani, capital of Province Orientale (900 km from Mboga), with the help of students from Mboga, including Ndahura Bezaleri and others attending the Université Libre du Congo in Kisangani.

In 1969, three Congolese priests were ordained in Mboga by Bishop Yonasani Rwakaikara of the Ruwenzori diocese. Tibafa Mugera, later Bishop of Kisangani; Rwahuire Mugarwa, later Archdeacon of Mboga; and Apando Yosiya.

Between 1960 and 1970, the Anglican Church of Congo expanded rapidly under Congolese leadership. Seven of the 8 tribes already evangelized by the EAC already had one or more priests. While the town of Béni had already been evangelized in 1968, it wasn't until 1970 that the EAC expanded into the territory of the same name. A year later, in 1971, the Butembo center was evangelized from Mboga.

Despite all this expansion, the Anglican Church still lacked competent personnel and sufficient and consistent material resources: no financial resources to meet the expenses of long-distance transport and administrative tasks. Many parishes didn't even have parish offices. The pastor sometimes spent more time walking long distances from his parish than he did in actual ministry. He lacked the time to learn more about his ministry, or even to reflect on a lively and understandable liturgy to rekindle the faith of his flock. He also lacked the time needed to strengthen the faith of Christians and to follow it up. Nevertheless, during this post-independence period, the Church showed its maturity by organizing its administration as best it could, and by leaving its homeland to take the Good News far and wide.

The Diocese of Mboga-Zaire monopolized the history of the Anglican Church for more than half a century. During this time, the Church remained confined to the rural areas of Mboga and the north-western part of Beni. There are three probable reasons for this:

Firstly, the 1910 Edinburgh Conference had assigned to the CMS an evangelizing field, more of which was located in the British colonies than in the French ones. Yet the Anglican Church could not flourish beyond its well-defined missionary sphere.

Secondly, in accordance with colonial legislation, Belgian colonists could not encourage missionary work by churches other than the Roman Catholic Church.

Finally, the inculturation of the tribalist gospel in and around Mboga. The Bahema and their neighbors, the Nande of Kainama, the Walendu Bindi, the Wanyali, the Watalinga and the Walese, made English Christianity their own religious heritage and kept it there. jealously guard their traditional cultural heritage. Indeed, as mentioned above, the catechism and the *Book of Common Prayer* (LPC) were written in Kihema (lunyoro) and imposed on other surrounding tribes until 1973, when the LPC was translated into Swahili. Thus, from 1896 to 1973, the Church was self-marginalized and radiated only within a sphere of more or less 80 km .[2]

To these three main reasons, we can add the question of identity. Because of the qualifier "Anglican", this Church initially appeared to be a specifically English affair, and consequently raised questions in the minds of the evangelized. This is one of the reasons why some countries have preferred to change the name "Anglican Church " to " Episcopal Church ".

desanglicize" Anglicanism. In the Democratic Republic of Congo, however, the EAC Executive Council decided to retain the name "Anglican Church".

6. Rapid growth in events

The erection of the Diocese of Mboga-Zaïre in 1972 accelerated the spread of the Gospel by the Anglican Church. For a variety of reasons, the Anglican Church underwent extraordinary expansion, with a massive influx of new Christians.

There were a large number of baptisms in the environment reached by the Anglican Church. The new converts discovered in this Church what had long remained unknown to them, and which corresponded to their aspirations: the emphasis placed on Bible reading, preaching and prayer, communion under its two species, confession of sins made directly to God and auricular confession at the request of the person concerned, and so on.

In addition, when in 1970 the State refused civil status to religious denominations whose legal organization or doctrines were not well defined, and these sought to join other denominations that already had civil status, the Anglican Church received many Christians from such denominations, particularly in the provinces of Kasai Oriental, Kasai Occidental, Katanga, the city of Kinshasa and the Maniema sub-region, with a view to instructing them in the Anglican faith.

In addition, with the freedom discovered at independence in 1960, the churches have also seen the movement of Christians from one church to another. The Anglican Church has welcomed Christians from other denominations, including the Roman Catholic Church, Pentecostal and other Reformed churches.

There's a flip side to every coin, and these massive new memberships have led to two important developments worth noting:

Firstly, there were very few pastors for such a large flock. The number of Christians was so disproportionate to the number of priests and evangelists that quality pastoral care was almost impossible. The problem of quantity was compounded by that of the quality of the evangelists: they were not sufficiently trained to cope with new situations, let alone to leave their usual environment to go and evangelize other tribes with customs and mores contrary to those of the evangelist. These evangelists, having no notion of ethnography or cultural anthropology, often came up against problems of misunderstanding.

Secondly, Christians from other denominations have a hard time forgetting what they learned from the catechism, theology or liturgy of their home churches, whose vision was often not the same as that of the host church. Those who were admitted en masse with their leader, for example, wanted to continue to remain under their leader's authority. They had difficulty obeying the pastor of the church that had received them. This led to a real struggle for leadership in the church. This situation sometimes took the Anglican Church to court. Such was the case in the Archdiaconate of Kananga, where a certain Kalala proclaimed himself Anglican Bishop and took the liberty of taking the Diocese of Bukavu, on which this Archdiaconate depended, to court on the grounds of encroaching on its rights, given that it was he who had entrusted these faithful to the Anglican Church. However, thanks to the dynamism of the Venerable Mudibwa and with the support of the Bukavu diocese, the Church won the case. Similarly, in Lubumbashi, a certain Sakambuya proclaimed himself Archbishop of the Anglican Church of Congo.

These quarrels persisted under Archbishop Ndahura Bezaleri, then Bishop of the Diocese of Bukavu. They continued under the bishops Dirokpa Fidèle and Mbona Kolini, who took charge of Katanga, and even became politicized under Mgr Henri Isingoma Kahwa, forcing him into exile in Limuru, Kenya, in 1999.

In view of all this turpitude, in 1986 the Executive Council of the Anglican Church demanded that people wishing to join the Anglican Church should do so as individuals and not as a group or association of individuals.

Finally, the Church was faced with problems of authority, doctrinal, structural and liturgical. It took good men to persuade people to change their views and adopt the Anglican tradition, through assiduous and effective teaching, but alas, this was not possible in most cases.

Nor should we lose sight of the tenacious attachment of many Africans to their customs and traditions, which also required judicious catechesis to ensure that the Church kept its Christian face, without necessarily waging a blind war on local culture. But African preachers, sometimes zealous, often continued with the iconoclasm of missionary times against traditional beliefs and customs, which was far from winning new followers to Christ.

All in all, in its rapid expansion, the Anglican Church has experienced a shortage in key areas of its life:

The shortage of human resources. As we have already pointed out, there was a crying shortage of qualified personnel to cope with the ever-increasing number of Christians. What's more, the Church, which had long operated in the bush, was now reaching out to the urban environment, made up of better-educated people who needed equally qualified instructors.

Shortage of material resources. The Church was also faced with the thorny problem of a lack of land for its building infrastructure: churches, residences for God's servants, especially in urban centers, so that sometimes we had to rent or be lodged by a generous Christian. There was also a shortage of basic necessities for worship, such as the Bible, the *Anglican Book of Common Prayer*, song books, etc., not to mention other needs that increased as the field of evangelization expanded: ecclesiastical vestments for worship, chalices, various registers, etc.

Shortage of financial resources. The Anglican Church found itself without any financial source to support the various pastoral and administrative burdens of the growing Church. Church leaders and Christians were doing their best, but this was far from meeting the needs of the growing Church. This situation of poverty was well noted by Canon Bill Norman, Commissioner of the Province of the Anglican Church of Congo (PEAC), Great Britain, at the celebration of the Church's Centenary on May 30, 1996, in Mboga: "The Anglican Church of Zaire is vigorous but very poor. The clergy are not paid in the true sense of the word. They live off the produce of their fields or as tent-makers. They don't expect to receive salaries from anywhere, but the Church does ask for help with development projects and scholarships, and with the salaries of some of its specialist staff such as secretaries, accountants and clerk-typists". (4)

7.   The Anglican Church of Congo within the Church of Christ in Congo (ECC)

On March 8, 1970, the Protestant Council of the Congo (CPC), of which the Anglican Church of the Congo (EAC) had been a member since 1956, became the Church of Christ in the Congo (ECC). The Anglican Church of Congo automatically became part of this new church.

The law of December 31, 1971 and its aftermath established the Eglise du Christ au Zaïre (ECZ) as the only recognized framework for the existence, presence and activities of Protestantism in the country.

Indeed, in 1910, the Edinburgh International Missionary Conference was the very important starting point for the regrouping of Protestant missions. The aim of this conference was to create a Protestant platform to resist the socio-religious discrimination of the colonial state, which was totally Catholic, and to delimit the field of evangelization in order to avoid conflict between the different denominations.

The Conseil Protestant du Congo was thus created in 1924 as a response to the recommendations of this conference. Protestants thus acquired a body to represent and defend their rights.

It should be pointed out that the CPC was a body with no power over members' missions; its authority was strictly consultative.

Whereas the Protestant Council of the Congo had only consultative powers, the Church of Christ in the Congo assumes legislative powers through its national and provincial synods. The administrative structure of the Church of Christ in the Congo is modelled on that of the Mouvement Populaire de la Révolution (MPR), President Mobutu's state party in Zaire. Church leaders at all levels bore the title of "President". The name *Eglise* was replaced by *Communauté,* preceded by the denomination's registration number in the Eglise du Christ au Zaïre (ECZ). For example: *ECZ-H^e Communauté Anglicane du Zaïre.* (The ECC is made up of 96 Communities, this year 2016, and the number is growing, every year, with the constant approval of new sects or certain members of the so-called Revival churches.

This reform, introduced by Bishop Bokeleale, then President of the ECC, was a brilliant idea to restore Protestant unity. Similar attempts succeeded in other countries such as India, Pakistan, etc., where several Protestant denominations - including the Anglican Church - agreed to form a single church: *Church of South India,   ChurchofNorthIndia   ,   ChurchofPakistan*, etc. Inthe1960s ,   these Christian denominations sat down together to examine their organizational structure and, above all, their respective doctrines and liturgies. In the end, they adopted what they considered to be good and right in each particular church, while making concessions in other areas. Thus, for example, the new Church adopted from the Anglicans the historic episcopate system and liturgical structure. The same initiative was successfully tried out by the *United Church of Canada,* made up of the Presbyterian,

Methodist and Congregational churches. However, it failed in Australia. Why ????

The reform of *the Church of Christ in the Congo* unfortunately stopped at administrative aspects, totally neglecting the theological, doctrinal and liturgical aspects, the very foundation of a Church. Such a reform was not without complicating the normal functioning of other Protestant denominations, who were quick to express their dissatisfaction with certain points.

On December 29, 1973, the Anglican Church of the Congo sent a memorandum to the ECZ because of its interference in the internal affairs of other churches.

Member churches, including the imposition of an administrative structure and disrespect for the tradition of other churches with "mother churches" abroad, the abandonment of the name *Anglican* Church for a simple Anglican Community, the obligation for Anglican faithful joining other Protestant denominations of the ECZ to be re-baptized, the accusation that the Anglican liturgy does not reflect the Reformation in its understanding of the doctrine of the Eucharist, the forced delimitation of the field of evangelization, etc. Added to this is the fact that some ECC communities do not baptize in water, in the name of the Holy Trinity (Mt 28:19; Jn 3:5). Finally, one wonders what kind of Church the Church of Christ in the Congo is, and what its doctrine is! It's based on a slogan: *"Unity in diversity", with* no respect for the specificity of member communities.

Given that all these circumstances placed the Anglican Church of Congo in an uncomfortable situation, by his letter n° CAZ/RL/474/81 of January 12, 1981, His Grace Ndahura Bezaleri, National Legal Representative of the EAZ, officially notified Bishop Bokeleale, National President of the ECZ, of the withdrawal of the Anglican Church of Zaire (EAZ) from the Church of Christ in Congo. This was done during the ECZ National Synod held in January 1981 at the Institut Bwindi in Bukavu.

After the official withdrawal of the EAZ from the ECZ, certain "adventurers" such as the Reverend Lumbala, a defrocked Anglican priest from Kinshasa, and his acolytes tried to replace the 11ᵉ Communauté Anglicane du Congo by the *11ᵉ /bis Communauté anglicane du Congo*, while appointing himself bishop of this "bis" community. In his efforts, he received the support and encouragement of certain ECZ leaders, but thanks to our vigilance, his efforts were a dead end. The Church of Christ in the Congo also accused the Anglican Church of the Congo of being a troublemaker within the Protestant communities, alleging that it was opposed to unity, and so on.

Following repeated requests from the ECZ, and conscious of its position as *via media* (middle way), the EAZ agreed to reintegrate the Church of Christ in Zaire. This decision was taken at the National Council meeting held in Lubumbashi on November 3, 1986, after the inauguration of the Diocese of Shaba.

On May 24, 1989, the College of Anglican Bishops notified the National Synod of the ECZ, held in Kinshasa on the above date, of the decision to reintegrate the Anglican Church of Zaire into the Church of Christ in Zaire.

The compromise reached stipulated that the ECZ should abandon all interference in the internal affairs of the Anglican Church of Zaire, which had an international structure within the worldwide Anglican Communion.

Relations between the Anglican Church of Congo and the Roman Catholic Church and other churches are good (Ps 133).

8. Management training

One of the solutions to the personnel shortage problems mentioned above was to equip the Church with sufficiently educated cadres to provide pastoral care in urban areas or large conurbations, take care of certain administrative duties and provide theological and biblical education in the dioceses and ecclesiastical province. Well-trained executives were also needed as chaplains in the country's primary and secondary schools, colleges and universities, hospitals and prisons.

However, the Anglican Church of Congo continued to train its pastors in Bible schools in Uganda, Kenya and Tanzania, where the language of training was Swahili, whereas the language of instruction in Congo is French. While Swahili is spoken in the eastern part of the country, French is spoken throughout. It is the language of communication with intellectuals and other people who have passed through school, even if only at primary level.

In this context, how could the pastors of the Anglican Church, established in all the provinces of the Congo, communicate with their faithful and all the intellectuals who frequented their community?

To remedy this situation and improve the image of God's servants, who appeared to be uneducated in their milieu of service, His Grace Ndahura Bezaleri, then Bishop of the Diocese of Bukavu and Archbishop of the Province of Burundi, Rwanda and Zaire, created *the Institut Théologique Interdiocésain* (I.T.I.) at secondary level in Bukavu on February 19, 1979. It offered theological and general courses in the national secondary school curriculum of Zaire. Its mission was to enable students to pass the State Examination and go on to university studies. The institute graduated two classes. The Reverend Meness, an American missionary, was Director of the I.T.I., and many of the teachers, including the Archbishop himself, provided quality teaching. But because of his insubordination to the Bishop, Reverend Meness was declared *persona non grata* and was hastily obliged to return to his home church, the Episcopal Church in the USA, in 1980, but the Institute continued to operate.

The institute was closed in 1982, after graduating one class. Some of these graduates were later ordained priests, such as Reverends Nkomero Ciri and Asaula.

The need to train pastors at university level was obvious. To this end, His Grace Ndahura Bezaleri *created the Institut Supérieur Théologique Anglican* (ISThA) in Bukavu on November 5, 1981. Only at graduate level, the ISThA initially received Congolese students from all dioceses, including Burundi, Madagascar and Guinea-Conakry. It only trained one class in Bukavu. The Reverend Dr. William Bailly (American Missionary of the Episcopal Church in the USA) was its first Director General.

After the unexpected death of His Grace Ndahura Bezaleri, the ISThA operated at the Bukavu diocesan center until the 1983-1984 academic year. Thereafter, it was closed
for budgetary reasons while students of the second promotion
were in their second year of graduation. In the meantime, its General Manager had to return to the United States at the end of his contract. The institute remained closed until 1987.

In 1986, for greater efficiency, the Executive Council of the Anglican Church of Congo decided that ISThA should be transferred from Bukavu to Bunia, close to the seat of legal representation, then under the Presidency of Mgr Patrice Njojo Byankya, Bishop of the Diocese of Boga, successor to His Grace Ndahura Bezaleri. The transfer took place in 1987, and the institute was placed under the direction of Reverend Jérémie Pemberton.

From 1989 onwards, the ISThA has offered a theology degree course and a Centre de Formation Biblique (CFB) for women students who do not have a state diploma, and for any other candidate wishing to receive biblical training. But budget constraints mean that the ISThA only produces an average of dozens of theology graduates a year, a drop in the ocean.

The creation of the ISThA to train the province's future executives was a highly commendable initiative, and the Church of Congo already has several graduates from this institute.

In fact, the Church needs to adapt to the current policy of Africanizing its leadership. The success of this policy will depend on the presence of people with sufficient intellectual baggage and quality, which will help them to take part in theological discussions or pastoral and liturgical reforms in which the African Churches, in search of a cultural identity of faith in Jesus Christ, are more involved than ever. With a better understanding of the cultural values of their co-religionists, they are expected to be able to devise messages that can truly touch the innermost depths of the Congolese people, and ensure in-depth evangelization and holistic ministry.

The creation of other training institutions followed in 2004: the Centre de Formation des Encadreurs pour la Jeunesse (CFEJ) in Mahagi, the Institut Supérieur de Technique d'Animation Sociale (ISTAS) in Mahagi, the Institut Supérieur Panafricain de Santé Communautaire (ISPASC) in Aru, the Institut Supérieur de Techniques Médicales (ISTM) in Aru, and so on.

9. The Anglican Church of Congo in the turmoil of political change in Congo

On November 24, 1965, General Joseph Désiré Mobutu's bloodless coup d'état put an end to Joseph Kasa-Vubu's presidency. This military putsch by the High Command of the Congolese

National Army (ANC) did not bring about any spectacular changes in the conduct and life of the Anglican Church until 1971.

On October 27, 1971, the Democratic Republic of Congo changed its name to the Republic of Zaire. A new flag and anthem were adopted.

national: the Zaïroise (replacing the Debout Congolais), the Congo River becomes the Zaïre River, and the Congolese currency will also be the "Zaïre". From now on, we'll speak of *37. i.e.:* the country, the river and the currency.

The Anglican Church of Congo or Communauté Anglicane du Congo (CAC) changes its name to Eglise Anglicane du Zaïre (EAZ) and later to Province de l'Eglise Anglicane du Zaïre (PEAZ) from 1992.

On February 15, 1972, a decision by the Political Bureau of the Mouvement Populaire de la Révolution (MPR), taken in the name of the policy of Recours à l'Authenticité, rejected Christian aliases and foreign names for towns, localities, tourist sites, lakes, rivers, soccer teams, etc., in favor of authentically Zairian names.

Religious denominations had to comply. Henceforth, the faithful were baptized with names of tribal or local authenticity. The liturgical calendar also changed, as all religious feasts falling within the weekday were postponed to Sunday or simply abolished (Christmas, Ascension, Assumption, Easter Monday, etc.).

10. Towards administrative and ecclesiastical autonomy for the Anglican Church of Mboga-Congo

10.1. Mboga Church in the Ecclesiastical Province of Uganda

April 16, 1961 saw the inauguration of the Ecclesiastical Province of Uganda, Burundi, Rwanda and Mboga-Congo, with administrative headquarters in Kampala, and the enthronement of its Archbishop His Grace Leslie W. Brown (a Briton). Meanwhile, the ecclesiastical district of Mboga remained under the jurisdiction of the Ugandan Diocese of Ruwenzori. Meanwhile, Uganda, still a British colony, only gained independence on October 9, 1962.

In 1965, Archbishop Erica Sabiti was enthroned as Archbishop of the Ecclesiastical Province of Uganda, Rwanda, Burundi and Mboga-Congo, replacing Leslie W. Brown. He is the first African from East Africa to be promoted to this position. The new Archbishop was also Bishop of the Diocese of Ruwenzori, to which the Anglican Church of Mboga-Congo belonged.

On February 16, 1977, His Grace Janani Luwum, then Archbishop for the Anglican Church of Mboga-Zaire as well, was assassinated in Kampala, by Ugandan President ldi Amin Dada because of his defense of Christian truth. He is considered a Saint Martyr in the Church of Uganda and also in the Anglican Church of Congo. A commemorative service in his honor is scheduled on this date in the *Anglican Book of Public Prayer* in Congo, as is the case for Saint Apolo Kivebulaya, whose commemorative service takes place on May 30 each year.

10.2. The creation of new parishes in the Mboga Church and autonomy for French-speaking countries

Since its creation, the Church of Mboga has grown steadily in number of faithful, chapels and parishes. New parishes were created: Geti in 1964, Bwakadi in 1965 and Bunyagwa in 1967. In 1970, other parishes were created, including Bunia, capital of the Ituri District, and Béni, capital of the Ituri Territory. In 1971, the Wanande parishes of Butembo, the Yira parish of Vuhozi and the Amba parish of Mulobya were created.

Despite this expansion, all major Church decisions were taken at diocesan synods held in Uganda, since the Mboga Church was part of this.

As one might expect, the concerns of the Congolese faithful could not be taken seriously, so it was necessary to wait for the inauguration of a Diocese in the DRC to acquire autonomy vis-à-vis the Diocese of Ruwenzori.

The Church of Uganda, which became an autonomous Ecclesiastical Province in 1961, ceded more and more responsibilities to the Congolese Church through the creation of *the Archdeaconry, Diocese.* In 1976, the *Francophone Council* was created within the Province of the Church of Uganda, Burundi, Rwanda and Zaire. Its aim was to grant a degree of autonomy (on the part of the Church of

English-speaking Uganda) to the French-speaking countries making up this Province, in order to deal with their affairs as Francophones and to better prepare an autonomous French-speaking Ecclesiastical Province.

The three French-speaking countries within the new (English-speaking) Ecclesiastical Province of Uganda were initially allowed to form the Conseil Francophone. In 1980, they regained their autonomy from the Church of Uganda and formed the autonomous French-speaking Ecclesiastical Province of Burundi, Rwanda and Zaire (PBRZ). The Anglican Church of Zaire finally became an autonomous Ecclesiastical Province in 1992: La Province de L'Eglise Anglicane du Zaïre (PEAZ), which led the Church of Congo to its Centenary.

10.3.   **The Church of Mboga: from Archdeaconry to Anglican Diocese**

The deanery of Boga, created in 1948, of which Mr. Rendle was the first Dean, replaced by a Ugandan, Reverend Walugyo, in 1960, was erected as an Archdeaconry in 1968. The Reverend Byakisaka Festo, appointed Canon by the Bishop of the Diocese of Ruwenzori a year earlier, became the first Archdeacon.

In 1969, the Reverend Theodore Lewis made a trip to Mboga and found a very well-organized Anglican Church. On his return to Kinshasa, he wrote a detailed report on the church. His report was widely circulated and used in Anglican circles around the world. One of the main grievances raised in the report was that of having a diocesan bishop in Congo to look after the Church. The matter was discussed at the Conference of Anglican Archbishops of the African Continent held in Zambia in February 1970.

At this meeting, the speakers recommended to the Archbishop of Uganda that an Anglican diocese be established in the Congo. Back in his diocese, the Bishop submitted the dossier to the diocesan synod, which approved the request. He then approached the CMS about the project and asked for an expatriate missionary to take on the role of first Anglican Bishop in the Congo. The CMS sent missionary Philip Ridsdale to head the very first Anglican Diocese of the Congo.

The Diocese was inaugurated on July 9, 1972 with the enthronement of Bishop Philp Ridsdale. At that time, there were 30 clergy, 25 parishes and 30 chapels (5).

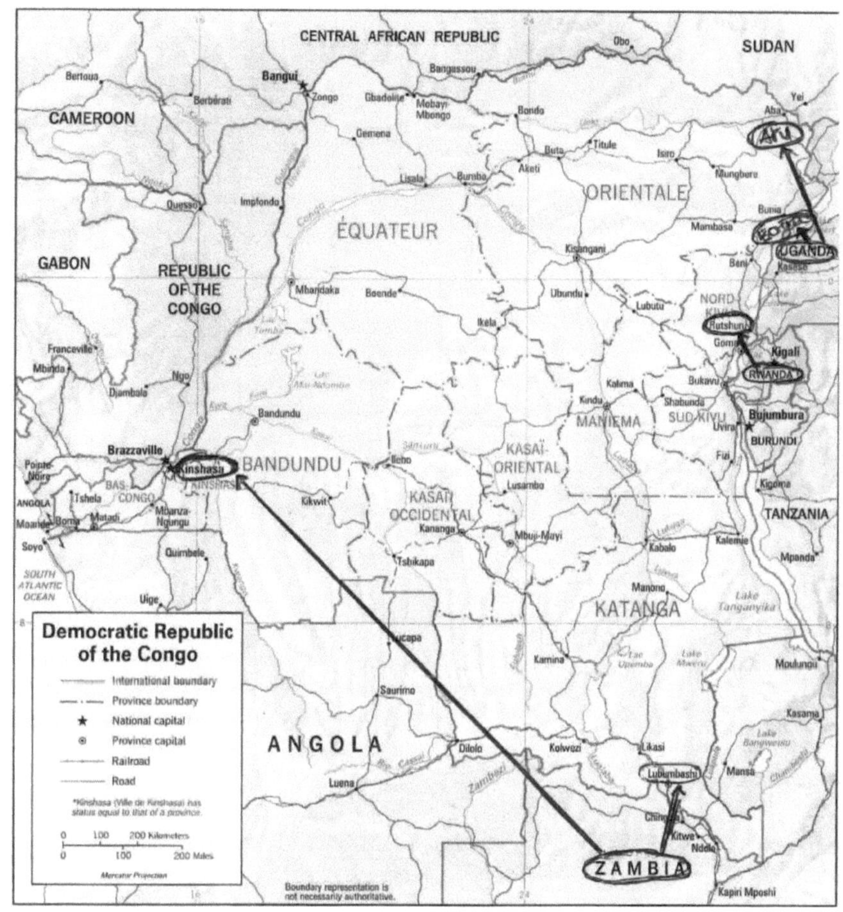

The different ways in which the Anglican Church enters the Congo

 Boga of Uganda in 1894

 Rutshuru / Masisi of Ruanda in 1934

 Lubumbashi (Elisabetville) from Zambia in 1950

 Kinshasa from Zambia in 1967

 - Aru! Mahagi from Uganda in 1979

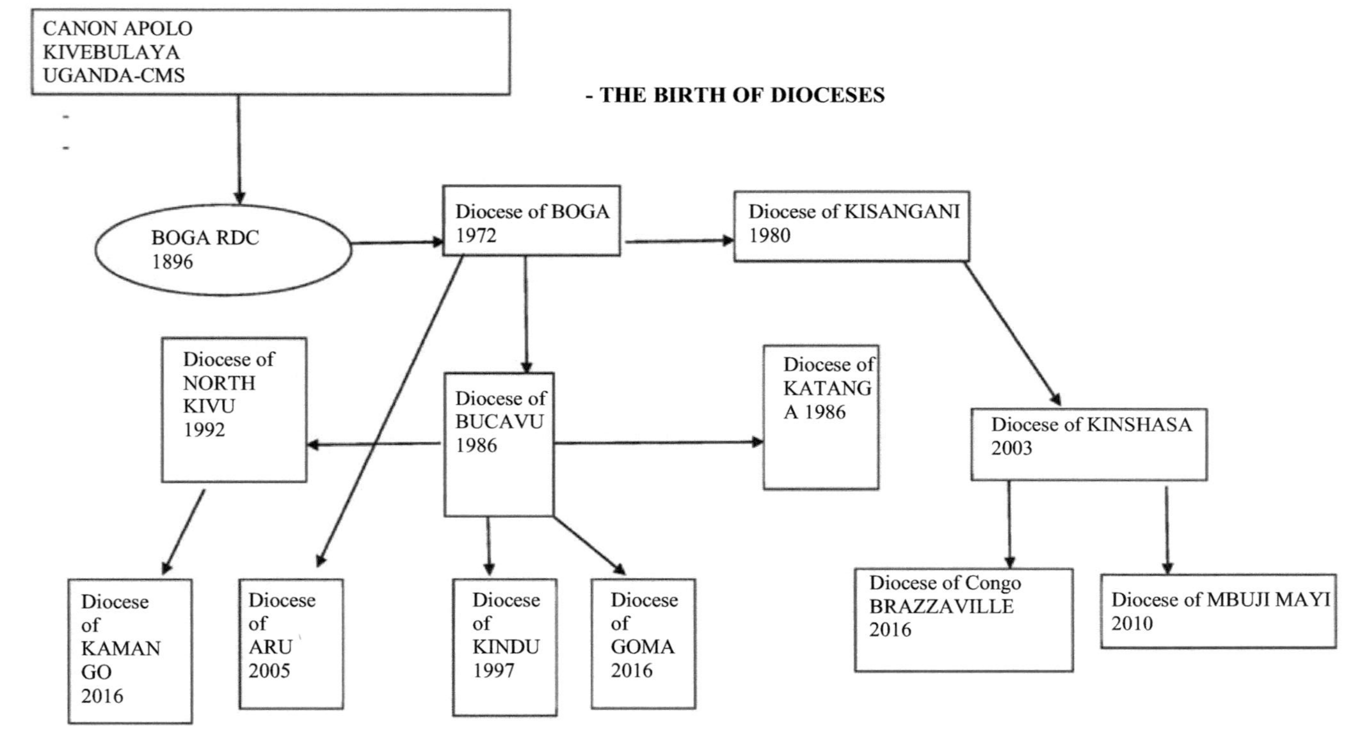

- THE BIRTH OF DIOCESES

CANON APOLO KIVEBULAYA UGANDA-CMS
BOGA RDC 1896
Diocese of BOGA 1972
Diocese of KISANGANI 1980
Diocese of NORTH KIVU 1992
Diocese of BUCAVU 1986
Diocese of KATANGA 1986
Diocese of KINSHASA 2003
Diocese of KAMANGO 2016
Diocese of ARU 2005
Diocese of KINDU 1997
Diocese of GOMA 2016
Diocese of Congo BRAZZAVILLE 2016
Diocese of MBUJI MAYI 2010

11. Diocese of Mboga-Zaire

Philip & Lucy Ridsdale
1972 - 1980

Patrice NJOJO BYANKIA &
KAMANYOHA
1980 -2007

Henri ISINGOMA KAHWA
2007 - 2009

William BAHEMUKA MUGENYI
2010 --

Located in the north-east of the Republic of Zaire, the Diocese of Mboga-Zaire had its headquarters in Mboga. Since its creation in 1972, it has been led by the following bishops: Philip Ridsdale, a British missionary with the CMS Church Missionary Society (19721980), Mgr Patrice Njojo Byankya, the first Zairian to head this Diocese (1980-2007), Mgr Henri Isingoma Kahwa (2007-2009) and Mgr William Bahemuka Mugenyi (2010-). When the Diocese of Mboga-Zaire was inaugurated, there were three archdeaconries: Mboga, Gety and Bunia.

The Diocese of Mboga-Zaïre currently has seven departments: Evangelization and Church Life, Mothers' Union, Sunday School, Youth Work (AGAPE), Theological Formation (ETE and Ecole Biblique), Community Development, Medical Services and Primary and Secondary Education. In carrying out its work, each department follows the two key principles of the Diocese: evangelization and social development.

Below are a few important events that recall the glorious past of this first Diocese of the Anglican Church of the Congo.

On March 2, 1973, Ndahura Bezaleri was ordained deacon at St. Apolo Kivebulaya Cathedral in Boga by Bishop Philip Ridsdale. In July 1974, he obtained his licentiate in theology from the Université Protestante du Congo (UPC) in Kinshasa. He was the first theology graduate from the EAC. On September 29 1974, he was ordained priest at St. Alban's Cathedral in England by Mgr Robert Runcie.

On August 24, 1975, Bishop Ndahura Bezaleri was consecrated Assistant Bishop of the Diocese of Mboga-Zaire. As such, he was the first Anglican Bishop of Zaire and the second Bishop of the EAZ.

On March 16, 1980, Mgr Njojo Byankya Patrice was ordained a priest at Christ Church Cathedral in Montreal, Canada, by Mgr Reginald Hollis, Bishop of Montreal.

Died December 25, 1981 in Bukavu, His Grace Ndahura Bezaleri, Bishop of Bukavu and Archbishop of the Province of Burundi, Rwanda and Zaire, was buried December 28, 1981 in Boga, next to the tomb of Apolo Kivebulaya.

On January 13, 1982, Bishop Njojo Byankya Patrice is elected National Legal Representative of the EAZ by the Church's National Council, replacing His Grace Ndahura Bezaleri. The EAZ administrative and head office moves from Bukavu to Mboga, Irumu zone, Haut-Zaire. His wife, Kamanyoha Njojo, was the first president of the Mothers' *Union* of the Diocese of Mboga-Zaire, whose secretariat was run by Madame Angonzebwa.

On April 7, 2007, His Grace Patrice Njojo retired. He died in Kampala on February 5, 2010, and was buried on February 7, 2010 next to the tomb of Apolo Kivebulaya, where the remains of His Grace Ndahura Bezaleri also lie.

The Archbishop of Canterbury, His Grace Williams Rowan, visited the Diocese of Boga from June 24 to 27, 2011, to appreciate the work of Apolo Kivebulaya, the Ugandan missionary and pioneer of the Anglican Church in Congo.

Since 1997, this diocese has been known as the Diocese of Boga.

12. Birth and development of other Congo dioceses

After the erection of the Diocese of Mboga-Zaire in 1972, new Dioceses were gradually created almost every 5 years. In 1996, the EAZ celebrated its centenary with five Dioceses: Mboga-Zaire, Bukavu, Kisangani, Shaba (Katanga) and Nord-Kivu.

Here is a brief biography of Bishop Philip Bullen Risdale, the first Bishop of the Diocese of Boga: he was born on 2-12-1915 and died on June 14, 2000. He married Lucy Barbauld Risdale on 24-6-1940, at Namirembe Cathedral, Kampala. He died at the age of 84. Lucy Barbauld Risdale was born on 18-9-1910 and died on December 9, 2011, aged 101. They are both buried in the garden of the Parish Church in Stapleford, Hertfordshire, England. Reverend Plilip B. Risdale was Parish Priest of this parish from 1964 - 1972; then Bishop of the Diocese of Boga-Zaire from 1972 - 1980.

IN LOVING MEMORY OF
PHILIP BULLEN
RIDSDALE
DIED 14 JUNE 2000
AGED 84
RECTOR OF THIS PARISH 1964-1972
BISHOP OF BOGA-ZAIRE 1972-1980
AND OF HIS WIFE
LUCY BARBAULD
RIDSDALE
DIED 9 DEC. 2011 AGED 101
"MY PRESENCE SHALL GO WITH THEE"
EXODUS 33 V.14

12.1. Diocese of Bukavu

NDAHURA BIZALERI
1976 - 1981

DIROKPA BALUFUGA FIDELE & MARIE RII KAHORO
1982 - 2006

In 1976, Bishop Ndahura Bezaleri arrived in Bukavu (800 km from Bunia), an area totally unknown to him. He was accompanied by Reverend Munzenda Musubaho Methusela and Evangelist Apimawa Jérôme.

The situation of the Diocese of Bukavu is a little peculiar, because almost always, the inauguration of a Diocese is preceded by the establishment of chapels, parishes and archdeaconries. But in the case of this Diocese, at the outset, the town of Bukavu had no Anglican Christians apart from the Bishop's family and close friends.

While his delegation was staying at the Cité, Mgr Ndahura was generously welcomed by the Archbishop of the Roman Catholic Church and Bishop of the Diocese of Bukavu, Mgr Mulindwa Mutabesha Aloys, who gave him temporary accommodation at the Procure Catholique Sainte Thérèse. Later, he found lodgings with a certain Mwanga Binusi at l'Essence, close to the present-day concession of St. Pierre Cathedral.

The Diocese of Bukavu was thus to devise a special evangelization program in the city and surrounding area, which was to lead to the rapid spread of the precepts of the Anglican Church.

On July 18, 1976, the Congo saw the birth of its second Diocese, that of Bukavu. Bishop Ndahura Bezaleri became the first diocesan bishop. He was consecrated and enthroned by His Grace Janani Luwum, Archbishop of the Church of Uganda, Burundi, Rwanda and Zaire, at the Kadutu stadium in Bukavu. And his wife Marjorie was the first President of the Mothers' *Union* of this enormous Diocese.

The Diocese of Bukavu is now on its third diocesan bishop. The late Bishop Bezaleri Ndahura was replaced by Bishop Dirokpa BalufUga Fidèle, consecrated and enthroned on February 21, 1982 by Bishop Sebununguri Adonia, Dean of the Province of Burundi, Rwanda and Zaire, Bishop Philip Ridsdale (EAZ First Bishop, retired) and Bishop Njojo Byankya Patrice, Bishop of the Diocese of Boga-Zaire and EAZ National Legal Representative (19822006). Bishop Dirokpa's consecration ceremonies took place at the Anglican Bishopric of Bukavu, in Muhumba. The third Bishop of this Diocese is Mgr Bahati Bali-Busane Sylvestre, consecrated and enthroned on December 3, 2006 by His Grace Dirokpa Balufiiga Fidèle at the Cathédrale St Pierre in Bukavu. He replaced the latter, who became Archbishop of the Province of the Anglican Church of Congo and Bishop of the Diocese of Kinshasa.

When the Anglican Church was first established in Bukavu, it encountered many difficulties on the part of the ecclesiastical leaders of the Church of Christ in Congo. The latter did not want the Anglican Church in Bukavu, which they felt should remain confined to Haut-Zaire (Province Orientale), contrary to the spirit of the Presidential Ordinance granting the Church Civil Personality and authorizing it to exercise its apostolate throughout the Republic. The Provincial President of the ECZ in South Kivu at the time, Rev. Emedi, had even prepared a letter for signature by the Kivu Regional Commissioner, to expel the Anglican Church from Bukavu.

However, having been warned of the ECZ's maneuvers, Bishop Bezaleri Ndahura immediately contacted the Regional Commissioner (Provincial Governor), armed with the aforementioned Ordinance, the contents of which had convinced this provincial authority.

Archbishop Ndahura succeeded in resolving the situation thanks to his vibrant appeal to the Commissioner of the Kivu region, who then issued an authorization for the Anglican Church to operate in his administrative entity, much to the astonishment of the regional authorities of the Church of Christ in Zaire.

When it was inaugurated, the jurisdiction of the Diocese of Bukavu covered the administrative regions of Kivu, Kasaï Oriental, Kasaï Occidental, Shaba and the city of Kinshasa. This made a total surface area of 1,058,682 Km^2, twice the size of France.

In all, the Diocese had only a few Christians. Following Apolo Kivebulava's earlier works, some churches already existed in the Kainama region of North Kivu. But thanks to the work of evangelization, the Church has spread to all the administrative regions listed above.

The evangelization undertaken by Mgr Ndahura in Masisi and Rutshuru in 1976 enabled the Church to recover its former members and its solid foothold in these territories. The Archdeaconry of Rutshuru, comprising the zones of Masisi, Rutshuru and Goma, was created to provide a framework for these Christians.

Bishop Ndahura Bezaleri was spiritual, intelligent, gifted, dynamic and visionary. He had a great concern for the development of the Anglican Church of Congo, in all areas.

On July 6, 1977, Mgr Ndahura Bezaleri, Bishop of the Diocese of Bukavu, took part in the National Synod of the Church of Christ in Zaire (ECZ) held at Lake Mukamba (Kasaï Oriental). On this occasion, he was approached by the leaders of certain sects such as Papa Kasea from Kasaï Oriental and Maman Mbombo Tshiala Anne from Kasaï Occidental. With a view to their integration into the Anglican Church of Congo. After the usual procedures, the EAZ Legal Representation Office in Boga granted their request, and their sects were converted into the Anglican Church. From 1978, the Anglican Church operated in Kasai Oriental under the leadership of Papa Kasea, and in Kasai Occidental under that of Mr. Mudibwa.

On May 11, 1980, the first French-speaking Province in Africa, "l'Eglise du Burundi, Rwanda et Zaïre" (PBRZ), was inaugurated in Bukavu. Bishop Ndahura Bezaleri of Bukavu was elected and enthroned as its first Archbishop. The archiepiscopal see was based in Bukavu.

On July 15, 1980, Dirokpa Balufuga Fidèle was elected Provincial Secretary by the first PEAZ Provincial Synod held in Bukavu. At the time, he was still an Evangelist in training for the diaconate in Boga, and would not be ordained a deacon until October 14, 1980 in the same locality, precisely at the Cathedral of St Apolo Kivebulaya, by the new Bishop of Mboga-Zaire, Mgr Njojo Byankya Patrice. This ordination took place on the Sunday following his consecration as Bishop of Boga, and was his first ordination service.

Following the ordination, Reverend Dirokpa B. Fidèle, accompanied by his entire family, immediately returned to his new post as Provincial Secretary of the Diocese of Bukavu.

On April 12, 1981, he was ordained a priest in Bukavu, in the Essence/Muhungu parish church, by His Grace Ndahura Bezaleri. That same year, he brought the Good News to Idjwi Island in Lake Kivu, where he knew no one. After intense evangelization, he opened an Anglican parish on the island, which is 80 km long and around 10 km wide, or 681 km^2, with a population of over 80,000 at the time. Today, the Anglican Church has opened 4 large parishes, 11 primary and secondary schools, 3 health centers, etc.

Following the sudden death of Archbishop Ndahura Bezaleri on December 25, 1981, Dirokpa Balufuga Fidèle was elected Bishop of the Diocese of Bukavu by the College of Bishops in Bukavu on January 15, 1982. He was consecrated and enthroned on February 21, 1982, as the second Bishop of the Diocese of Bukavu.

On November 7, 1982, Bishop Dirokpa B. Fidèle ordained the first deacons for the Anglican Church of the two Kasais in Bukavu. They were Reverend Mudibwa Tshongo for Kasaï Occidental and Mukendi Mpinga Casimir for Kasaï Oriental.

With a view to strengthening its ministry to the faithful, the Diocese of Bukavu has placed particular emphasis on training in basic theology, improving church life, structuring Bible schools, theological education by extension (TEE), *cassette* ministry (easy to handle by anyone), Sunday school for children, group Bible study, etc. The Diocese of Bukavu is also involved in the development of theological education by extension (TEE).

Nor had the Diocese of Bukavu forgotten the holistic aspect of its ministry. Several departments were thus created in the Diocese, with their ramifications, as far as possible, in all the archdeaconries and parishes. These included: evangelization, education, theological training, church life, community development office, medical service, youth, the *Mothers'* Union, whose second president, Mama Marie Rii Kahoro Dirokpa, was appointed in 1982,   and   social development   projects   .

encouraged the growth of the Diocese and contributed to the creation of a number of parishes and archdeaconries (Bukavu, Kindu, Shaba, Goma, Kasaï Oriental, Kasaï Occidental, etc.).

In all these evangelization and training activities, the Diocese of Bukavu had always been supported by the CMS/England, which was assisted by a large number of missionaries from the CMS/Australia from 1987 to 1996. They worked and rendered valuable services at the Bukavu diocesan center, then at Butembo and Kindu, which were archdeaconries of the Bukavu diocese.

On February 9, 2004, death snatched Maman Marie Rii Kahoro, wife of His Grace Dirokpa B. Fidèle, from our affections. Fidèle. She was buried in the garden of Bukavu's Cathédrale St Pierre on February 12, 2004.

In April 1994, during the unfortunate events in the Republic of Rwanda, the Diocese of Bukavu was invaded by a large number of Rwandan refugees, initially Tutsi, following the assassination of President Habyarimana Juvénal, whose plane was shot down in mid-flight (the Burundian President Cyprien Ntaryamiras was also on board the plane). same plane), then Hutus, from July 1994. At the Bukavu diocesan center, 3,000 Hutus occupied the Bishop's compound in Muhumba and 7,000 were received in and around Bukavu's Cathedral Saint Pierre. When thousands of Hutu refugees burst into Bukavu, the Tutsis had returned to Rwanda. The drama of the refugees at the Bishop's Palace and Cathedral lasted two weeks. During this period, they had to be asked to clear the interior of the Cathedral so that Sunday worship could take place. At the end of the two-week period, they all moved to the various reception sites prepared by the UNHCR with the help of the local government. The Anglican Church of Congo continued to be in contact with Anglican refugees in the various camps.

Welcoming these large numbers of refugees also destroyed some of the Church's infrastructure: trees were ruthlessly cut down and allowed into the Church's concession for firewood. The same applied to school and chapel benches, etc.

Apart from many small refugee camps, the Diocese of Bukavu has seen two vast camps: Kashusha, 25 km from the city of Bukavu, and Mugunga, 10 km from the city of Goma, with over half a million refugees each. These refugees were dispersed in October 1996 by the AFDL (Alliance des Forces Démocratiques pour la Libération du Congo-Zaïre) army, made up of Ugandan, Rwandan, Burundian and Congolese soldiers. This army, under the leadership of Laurent Désiré Kabila, took over Kinshasa, the capital of Zaire, on May 17, 1997, putting an end to the 32-year dictatorship of President Mobutu Sese Seko.

On the occasion of its 25th anniversary, the Diocese of Bukavu presented certificates of fidelity to all those who had faithfully served the Church. On this occasion, lay people such as Papa Kayungu Ambroise and Mama Viviane Semugeshi were appointed Canons.

The Diocese of Bukavu also remains grateful to all those who were active among its first followers. These include :
1. Mr Walumona Bisikongo who was a Church Elder
2. Mr Bekilwa Mwanda (still alive)
3. Mr Bilangaliza Walumona Gilbert, current BDC/Bukavu Deputy Diocesan Coordinator
4. Ev Kubali Njamako Kakunda (deceased)
5. Mr Ichukwe Kondekelwa Jean (deceased)
6. Chan Kayungu Lwamba Ambroise (still alive)
7. Mama Bitondo Shabani
8. Mr Mushingilwa Bulele (still alive)

On the other hand, among those who supported the Church and whose names we still remember, there are :
1. Papa Milinganyo, then Church Elder 8ᵉ CEPAC/Sayuni, who sold us the Pastor's house in Essence.
2. Mwanga Yunusi, who had housed Archbishop Ndahura's family in his house in Essence before the Church bought the bishop's current residence in Muhumba.
3. The Military Auditor of the time, who had facilitated the occupation and peaceful enjoyment of the Muhumba concession, purchased from Mr Boulanger and which the military had occupied anarchically.

We would also like to mention the great services rendered to this Diocese by our missionaries: the Reverend Richard Menees, Miss Susan L. Broddus of the Episcopal Church USA, the couple Mr Folkerts, the Reverend Dr William Belly, Miss Louise Wright of CMS England, the Venerable Linus Njuki of Kenya, the Reverend Charles of Uganda, the couple David Boyds of CMSA), Geoff

Stanbury, Margaret Lawry, Bill Visser, Mgr Peter Dawson, the couple Richard Malcholm, the Georges Pitt family, Miss Sarah Beckstrom. [See attached list] of CMS/Australia missionaries who have worked in the Anglican Church of the Congo].

The Diocese of Katanga (then Shaba) was inaugurated on November 2, 1986, with the enthronement of Bishop Emmanuel Mbona Kolini as its first Bishop. The Diocese of North Kivu was inaugurated on February 23, 1992, with the consecration of Bishop Methusela Munzenda Musubaho as its first Bishop.

In the same year, on February 2, 1992, Mgr Peter Dawson of CMS/Australia was consecrated Assistant Bishop of the Diocese of Bukavu at Saint André Cathedral in Sydney, New South Wales, by His Grace Donald Robinson, Archbishop and Bishop of the Diocese of Sydney, Australia. He was sent to Kindu in 1992 to prepare the new Diocese of Kindu, which was inaugurated on August 31, 1997, with the consecration of Bishop Zacharie Masimango Katanda as titular bishop.

As for the Archdeaconries of the two Kasais, which were part of the Diocese of Bukavu for 25 years (1978-2003), they requested, during the EAC Provincial Synod held in Bukavu in February 2003, their detachment from the Diocese of Bukavu in order to join the new Diocese of Kinshasa. The reason seemed to be twofold: on the one hand, Kinshasa is closer than Bukavu and easier to reach; on the other, as the former Bishop of Bukavu had become Archbishop and Bishop of the new Diocese of Kinshasa, they preferred to follow their former pastor, with whom they had already started the race against time to prepare the Diocese of Kasaï. The new Diocese of Kasaï was inaugurated in Mbuji-Mayi on January 30, 2011, with the enthronement of Bishop Kapinga Marcel as its first Bishop.

We can thus confirm that the Diocese of Bukavu has given birth to the 4 Dioceses of the EAC, and is now preparing a fifth Diocese, that of Goma.

Transferred to the Diocese of Kinshasa in 2003, Bishop Dirokpa BalufUga Fidèle convened the diocesan synod of Bukavu in 2004 to elect his successor. This dossier was presented to the College of Bishops meeting in Kinshas in early 2005, but following unjustified complaints from a candidate who had failed miserably in the elections, the College demanded that the same election be held again in a year's time, under the supervision of another president of the synod, assisted by observers from other sister churches in Congo and Rwanda. Meanwhile, the Bishop of Bukavu was replaced by the Venerable Ise-Somo of the Diocese of North Kivu, still under the supervision of Bishop Dirokpa B. Fidèle. Fidèle. At the beginning of 2006,   another synod was   convened   , as required by the Bishops' Collegium   .
members of this synod voted unanimously for the same contested candidate, in the person of the Venerable Bahati-Bali Busane Sylvestre.

The result of the ballot was presented to the College of Bishops, who ratified it without a hitch, and Venerable Bahati-Bali Busane was consecrated and enthroned on December 3, 2006, as the third Bishop of the Diocese of Bukavu. His wife, Mama Veneranda Nyota BAHATI, has been President of the Union des Mères since 2006, replacing Mama Marie Rii Kahoro Dirokpa, who died in 2004.

From 2003 to 2006, Bishop Dirokpa Balufuga Fidèle managed two Dioceses at the same time, that of Bukavu and that of Kinshasa. He headed the Diocese of Bukavu for 24 years (1982-2006).

The Diocese of Bukavu currently operates 12 departments: Evangelization, Christian Education, School Chaplaincy, AGAPE Christian Youth, Mothers' Union, Community Development Office, Medical Service, Teaching, Executive Training, Finance and Stewardship, Public Relations and Bible School Training (3 Bible Schools: Kiwandja, Bangwe and Bukavu).

Projects currently active in the Diocese include the Anglican Peace Center, the Cyber Café (Internet), support for women survivors, 10 health centers and 2 hospitals, the Panda Center, the Bagira multi-purpose hall, the motorboat on Lake Kivu and adult literacy.

There are 11 archdeaconries in this diocese: Bukavu, Goma, Uvira, Lake Kivu (Kalehe), Lake Tanganyika (Baraka), Itombwe, Masisi, Rutshuru, Walungu, Bunyakiri and Binza (Nyamilima).

The number of Anglican schools in the Diocese of Bukavu is 129, comprising 84 elementary school and 42 secondary schools, including 3 vocational schools.

### 12.2.	Diocese of Kisangani

TIBAFA MUGERA Sylvestre
1980 - 2000

FUNGA BOTOLOME Lambert
2000 -

The Diocese of Kisangani was inaugurated on October 12, 1980 with the enthronement of Bishop Mugera Tibafa Sylvestre as its first Bishop by His Grace Ndahura Bezaleri, Archbishop of the Province of Burundi, Rwanda and Zaire. On this occasion, Archbishop Philip Ridsdale, on whom the Archdeaconry of Kisangani depended, retired on the same day. Bishop Mugera Tibafa Sylvestre was consecrated in Boga on October 7, 1980. The Diocese of Kisangani is thus the third Diocese of the Anglican Church of Congo.

Mgr Tibafa Mugera Sylvestre, having reached the retirement age stipulated by the PEAC Constitution, was ready to retire. Death snatched him from our affection and that of the Church, on October 6, 2000, in Kisangani. His funeral took place on October 10, 2000, in the Cathedral of St Jean in the Diocese of Kisangani. He died before beginning his retirement and before the enthronement of his successor.

His successor will be Bishop Funga Batolome Lambert. Bishop Lambert was consecrated on September   10, 2000   at Saint   Apolo Cathedral in Boga   .
of Bishop of the Diocese of Kisangani on December 15, 2000 at the Cathédrale St Jean de Kisangani by His Grace Patrice Njojo Byankya.

The Diocese of Kisangani arose from the division of the Diocese of Boga-Zaire. It is located in the north-east of the Republic of Zaire. At the time, it covered the administrative sub-regions of Kisangani, Tshopo, Bas-Uélé, Haut-Uele and the capital of Kinshasa (from 1981 to 2002).

Initially, members of the Anglican Church of Kisangani consisted of defectors from a sect called "L'Eglise Indépendante du Congo Central" (EICC) and the "Baptist Missionary Society" (BMS). At the time, they were under the supervision of Reverend Bezaleri Ndahura, a student at the Kisangani university campus. Some time after the birth of this new community, Bishop Philip Ridsdale of the Diocese of Boga-Zaire sent a permanent servant to the Church of Kisangani in the person of Reverend Sylvestre Tibafa Mugera. He began work as the parish's first parish priest in February 1973. Immediately, he set up a program of evangelization and teaching of Anglican doctrine and liturgy.

In the same year, he established two parishes in Kabondo and Lubunga, without the city of Kisangani. On March 18, 1973, the Christians celebrated the baptism of 59 people. Following this, 93 people received confirmation at the hands of Bishop Philip Risdale. In 1974, three further parishes were established in Yalokombe, Yamofaya and Matete.

The first local deacons, Reverends Likunde and Ndeke Nhelo, were ordained on May 01, 1975. In the same month, Reverend Tibafa was appointed Archdeacon of Kisangani, with jurisdiction over five parishes. A year later, Reverend Botomoito Asoyo was also ordained.

The Lord's work had expanded remarkably. The number of Christians grew rapidly, and new parishes and archdeaconries were created, culminating in the decision to inaugurate an autonomous diocese with Kisangani as its center, which took place on December 10, 1980.

Before the EAZ centenary in 1996, the Diocese of Kisangani had some 6,500 members grouped in four archdeaconries (Kisangani, Kinshasa, Yomofaya and Bolingo) comprising 37 parishes served by 39 priests.

The Diocese of Kisangani had carried out several projects. These included the creation of 33 primary and secondary schools, 2 dispensaries, a development office, a Bible school and the construction of several buildings, including the Cathedral of St. John, the diocesan administrative office, the Mothers' Union office and the welcome center.

However, these works were not accomplished without certain difficulties. Firstly, Reverend Tibafa found it difficult to train committed Anglican Christians, because the first members came from communities whose doctrines were fundamentally different from Anglicanism. In addition, the Church's expansion within the Diocese was thwarted by other religious groups such as the BMS (Baptist Missionary Society) and the U.F.M. (Unevangelised Field Mission). Finally, the deplorable state of the roads often prevented pastoral visits.

To enable the work already begun in the Diocese to continue, certain important tasks needed to be accomplished, such as the creation of a new Diocese in Kinshasa, the training of qualified personnel to advance the work of the various departments, support for the formation of young people and the reshaping of the method of evangelization.

On December 14, 1997, the Venerable Mavatikwa Kany was consecrated Assistant Bishop of the Diocese of Kisangani, with residence in Kinshasa, at the Cathédrale saint Jean de Kisangani. His mission was to prepare the future Diocese of Kinshasa. Sadly, Bishop Mavatikwa Kany passed away prematurely on December 29, 1999 in Kinshasa , and was buried in the garden of the Protestant Centenary Cathedral in Kinshasa.
Kinshasa.

Mgr Tibafa Mugera Sylvestre, having reached the retirement age stipulated by the PEAC Constitution, was ready to retire. Death snatched him from our affection and that of the Church, on October 6, 2000, in Kisangani. His funeral took place on October 10, 2000, in the Cathedral of St Jean in the Diocese of Kisangani. He died before beginning his retirement and before the enthronement of his successor.

On December 20, 2003, the Archdiaconate of Kinshasa separated from the Diocese of Kisangani to become an autonomous diocese.

On June 3, 2006, Maman Kamanda Funga, the second President of the *Mothers' Union* and wife of Mgr Funga Batolome Lambert died in Kisangani. Her funeral took place on June 04, 2006 in the garden of the Cathédrale Saint Jean in Kisangani.

Emmanuel MBONA KOLINI
1986 - 1997

Henri ISINGOMA KAHWA
1997 - 2007

Corneille KASIMA MUNO
2006 -2016

ELISHA TENDWA
Assist Kalemie 2012 -

BERTIN MWALE SUBI
2016 -

The Anglican Church's mission in Katanga began with the Anglican Church of Zambia, formerly Northern Rhodesia, supported by the British mission in London, USPG (United Society for Propagating the Gospel).

Between 1950 and 1955, Bishop Ronald Owen extended his diocese beyond the Congolese border to provide pastoral care for Zambian Anglican families (especially from the Bemba tribe, originally from Zambia) working for the Union Minière du Haut Katanga in Elisabethville, now Lubumbashi.

Sebastian Chungupengu, the very first catechist, served the Church from 1954 until the troubled years of I960, which led to a marked decline in the number of Christians.

A chapel was bought from German Lutherans in 1958 on the road to Kafubu, in the commune of Kampemba, today the Paroisse Saint André, which in 1986 was the smallest cathedral in the Anglican Communion, with barely 25 pews.

In I960, the Katanga war of secession led to a mass exodus of church members to Zambia. The small indigenous community that remained was led by catechist Pascal Chamfya. It should be noted that this Anglican Church of Elisabethville was ignored by the official Anglican Church of North-East Congo, whose headquarters were in Mboga.

In 1972, a presidential decree was promulgated prohibiting the existence of churches not officially recognized by the Congolese state. Subsequently, when the Protestant churches were grouped under a single ecclesiastical organization called the "Church of Christ in Zaire", certain religious sects in Lubumbashi, affected by this measure, sought integration into the Anglican Church of Congo, headquartered in Bukavu. Archbishop Ndahura Bezaleri accepted this request.

In1980   ,   BishopNdahuraBezalerien   invited   BishopEmmanuelMbonaKolini   .

Assistant in the Diocese of Bukavu, Katanga, where he arrived on August 31, 1981. His main objective was to train the leaders of the integrated sects to teach the Anglican catechism to all new adherents. His mission was also to prepare the fUtur Diocese of Shaba.

The inauguration of the Diocese of Shaba, which is the 4^e Diocese of the PEAC, took place on November 2, 1986 in Lubumbashi, with the enthronement of Bishop Mbona Kolini Emmanuel as its first Bishop. The enthronement ceremonies took place in the June 30 building in Lubumbashi. They were presided over by His Grace Njojo P. Byankya, Archbishop of the PEAC. This diocese is located in the cobalt and copper mining area of southern Zaire, with its headquarters in the regional capital Lubumbashi.

In 1997, Mgr Mbona Kolini Emmanuel fled to Rwanda, following the unhealthy political situation in   Katang   Province, renowned   for   its ethnic   and religious divide.

xenophobia in full swing. He was replaced by Bishop Henri Isingoma Kahwa. The latter was consecrated and enthroned as second Bishop of the Diocese of Katanga on September 11, 1997 by His Grace Njojo P. Byankya, Archbishop of the PEAC.

Given that Bishop Patrice Njojo Byankya of Boga was due to retire and the seat was vacant, the Extraordinary Synod of the PEAC held on September 30, 2006, decided that Bishop Henri Isingoma Kahwa of Katanga should be transferred to the Diocese of Boga. A new Bishop of the Diocese of Katanga was then elected.

The choice fell on the Reverend Kasima Muno Corneille, who was consecrated and enthroned on November 26, 2006 at Saint Paul de la Kenya Cathedral in Lubumbashi by His Grace Dirokpa Balufuga Fidèle, Archbishop of the PEAC. He is the third Bishop of the Diocese of Katanga.

On this occasion, the Cathedral was blessed and officially opened by His Grace Dirokpa Balufuga, replacing the small Cathedral of Saint André in Lubumbashi.

To facilitate administration and given the size of the Diocese of Katanga, it was decided at the 6eme diocesan synod held from July 19 to 23, 2010 in Lubumbashi, to create an assistancy based in Kalemie. For this reason, Assistant Bishop Mgr. Elisha Tendwa, a missionary from the Anglican Church of Tanzania, was consecrated Bishop on November 25, 2012 at Saint Paul's Cathedral in Kenya by His Grace Henri Isingoma Kahwa.

In the centenary year of the Anglican Church of Zaire (1996), the Diocese of Shaba celebrated its 10eme anniversary.

The Diocese of Katanga has carried out a number of projects. In the 1980s, it built a diocesan residential training center in Lubumbashi, a health center in Kaniama, a development office and an education office.

In the early 1990s, "the city of Lubumbashi was severely affected by the social unrest in Zaire during the looting of early 1990 and 1992. The looting of September 1991 forced   expatriates   to   leave   the country   . Katangese (natives) and Kasaians who had been brought in to work in the mines. The Kasaians, among whom were many Anglicans, were forced to leave Katanga, and as a result, the church membership was halved"(6).

In the two Kasais, on the other hand, the number of Anglican worshippers had fallen considerably, creating a   real bottleneck for the churches, which   ,   lacking were unable to provide effective support for the large number of refugees, especially as many of them lacked host families.

Despite this, the Church's ministry continued, especially that of leadership training, not only for pastors, deacons and evangelists, but also for Sunday school, youth training and the Mothers' Union. This training has provided the Church with a solid foundation and smoothed out many doctrinal difficulties. Lay training has equipped the Church with people ready to share the responsibilities of ministry. The Church's social ministry has also developed. Seminars on preventive health care, the nutrition program and the creation of dispensaries were given priority in the health field.

The Development Office has encouraged small-scale farming and organized workshops for learning new techniques. As the Diocese of Shaba looks to the future, its vision is to encourage evangelization, regeneration and the ministry of peace, justice and reconciliation.

The Anglican Community Development Office (BDC) works with a Rural Infrastructure Development Support Project (PADIR). This project is financed by the African Development Bank (ADB). It is implemented by the Anglican BDC as a Local Executing Agency (LEA) in the four provinces of Katanga.

In terms of youth training, the Diocese has built 48 primary and 20 secondary schools. As a result, the resident advisor for these schools has been promoted to Anglican Schools Coordinator.

A center called the *Kimbilio Center* has been set up to care for *street* children. Officially inaugurated on July 17, 2009, the Kimbilio center accommodates 17 boys, 11 of whom are housed there and 6 in the transit house. There is also a shelter for girls from broken homes, accommodating 6 girls. A home for these girls is currently under construction, and they will soon be able to move into it. In addition, 46 children are cared for in the day center.

The British missionary lan Harvey who was in charge of the Kimbilio Center has ended his mission since 2013 in Congo and is replaced by Tshiswaka Jean Bosco who was appointed by CMS as local missionary.

NB. The list of missionaries who have worked in the Katanga diocese can be found in table no. 1 in the appendix to this work.

The Diocese of Katanga maintains the following offices: Union des Mères (U.M.), Bureau de Développement Communautaire (BDC), Institut Biblique Anglican St Paul (IBAP), Primary and Secondary Education, Community Health (SACOM), Jeunesse Chrétienne Agape (JCA), Evangelization and Shirika la Andrea Mutakatifu (SHAM) or Lay Ministry.

A total of 10 archdeaconries, 1 deanery, 45 parishes, 45 ordained pastors and 10,900 Christians: this is the result of the work carried out by the Diocese of Katanga up to 2015.

In this Anglican ecclesiastical body, retired Canon Mukendi Kamanda Raphaël is the Congolese who has played the most important role in its history. The President of the Union des Mères is Mme Pacifique Kasima. Bishop KasimaMuno Corneille will retire in August 2016.

The Diocese of Katanga will celebrate the thirtieth anniversary of its creation on November 2, 2016. It is currently preparing for the erection of the Diocese of Kalemie, to which the Assistant

Bishop, Mgr ElishaTendwa, has been assigned.

12.4. Diocese of North Kivu

MUNZENDA MUSUBAHO METHUSELA & Son Epouse
1992 - 2008

KAYEEYE ENOCK
Ass Nord Kivu 2006 - 2010

ISE-SOMO
2010 -

The Diocese of North Kivu, which is the 5ᵉ EAZ Diocese, was inaugurated on February 23, 1992 with the consecration and enthronement of Bishop Musubaho Munzenda Methusela in the Cathedral of Saint André in Butembo by His Grace Samuel Sindamuka, Archbishop of the Province of Burundi, Rwanda and Zaire (PBRZ). He is thus the first Bishop of this Diocese, which arose from the division of the Diocese of Bukavu.

The Diocese of North Kivu is located in eastern Zaire, in the Province of North Kivu. However, the southern part of the Province of North Kivu remains attached to the Diocese of Bukavu, from Kanyabayonga to Goma, including the administrative areas of Masisi, Rutshuru and Goma.

The Diocese of North Kivu comprises the territories of Beni and Lubero. The Diocese originally comprised 3 Archdeaconries: Beni, Butembo and Watalinga. In 1987, this entity benefited from the presence of a number of Australian missionary couples, thanks to the efforts of His Excellency Dirokpa Balufuga Fidèle, then Bishop of the Diocese of Bukavu. The presence of missionary couples Reverend Fagan and Ruth Brian, Dr Brett and Raya Newell, Dentist Graham and Wendy Toulmin, Malcolm and Sheilly was a great opportunity for the growth of the Church in the fields of evangelization and development. Unfortunately, these missionaries left Zaire against their will, following the troubles of the early 1990s.

From 1999 onwards, a leadership conflict tore the Diocese of North Kivu apart. This prompted the College of Bishops meeting in Kampala to suspend Bishop Munzenda and appoint the Venerable Canon Bahati Bali-Busane Sylvestre of the Diocese of Bukavu as Vicar General, with the task of reconciling and mediating between the conflicting groups.

This conflict lasted until 2001, when Bishop Munzenda's suspension was lifted and Canon Enock Kayeeye was appointed assistant bishop of the diocese. His consecration as Bishop was celebrated in Butembo on October 22, 2006 by His Grace Archbishop Dirokpa Balufuga Fidèle. It was during this period that many new parishes and archdeaconries were created in the diocese.

The Diocese of North Kivu is now at its 2ᵉ Bishop, in the person of Mgr Ise-Somo Muhindo, who replaced Mgr Munzenda Musubaho, who retired in 2008. He was consecrated and enthroned on December 12, 2010 on the grounds of the Anglican school, in front of the Cathedral of Saint André in Butembo, by His Grace Henri Isignoma Kahwa, Archbishop of the PEAC when the conflict was in full swing in this Diocese. Glory be to God for the wisdom he gave to his servant Mgr Ise-Somo to manage the conflict, which has finally come to an end without bloodshed.

This Diocese comprises the oldest parishes of the Diocese of Bukavu, from which it separated in 1992. Apolo Kivebulaya opened the first Anglican chapel in North Kivu at Kainama in 1921. In 1937, the Kainama parish was inaugurated. In the same year, the parish of Kamango (Watalinga) was created [autonomous diocese as of 2016]. In 1939, an attempt was made to introduce Anglicanism into Lubero Territory. In the wake of this, Samuel Buhese Makenze, a Congolese catechist who had long lived in Uganda, opened an Anglican church in Kigheri (Kambali / Butembo) on his return home. However, he was harassed by Baptist missionaries from the CEBK (Communauté des Eglises Baptistes du Kivu) and imprisoned with two colleagues for ten years.

After this setback, Butembo waited until 1969 for the Anglican Church to be re-established under the supervision of evangelists from Kainama. By 1974, other evangelists, also from Kainama, were working in Mbau, where the Diocese of North Kivu has a Bible school.

Today, the diocese has 6 archdeaconries: Butembo, Beni, Watalinga, Rwenzori, Kainama and Basongora, with 35 parishes. It has 9 departments: evangelization, community development, medical service, teaching, cassette ministry, youth, Sunday school and Christian education, and the Mothers' Union, whose first President was Mama Munzenda, now replaced by Mama Ise-Somo.

Vital importance is attached to education at all levels. Several Church leaders have studied at various Christian institutions, while training seminars are organized in parishes for Church members.

The Diocese wishes to pursue its education projects and open more primary, secondary and technical schools to ensure a comprehensive education worthy of tomorrow's world.

The Diocese of North Kivu was the first Diocese in the PEAC to ordain an Anglican woman to the priesthood, in the person of Reverend Joyce Muhindo, in 2003, at the Cathedral of Saint André in Butembo, by Bishop Muzenda Musubaho Methusela.

The Diocese of North Kivu, following the detachment of the Archdeaconry of Watalinga, gave birth to a new autonomous Diocese of Kamango on January 31, 2016, whose titular Bishop is Bishop Daniel Sabiti Tibafa.

Mgr Munzenda Musubaho Methusela died on December 3, 2011 in Beni. He was buried on December 5, 2011 in the garden of the parish church of Saint Jean de Kasabinyole in Beni.

The Diocese of North Kivu currently boasts 41 parishes, 83 pastors, 10124 faithful, 11 archdeaconries, 152 primary and secondary schools, 2 new universities: Université Anglicane Apolo Kivebulaya (UAAKi) in Butembo and Université Anglicane en Afrique Centrale (UNAAC) in Beni, 25 health facilities and 1 dental clinic.

13. The development of Anglican liturgy in the Congo
- 3.1. The lunyoro liturgy

The liturgy used by Apolo Kivebulaya, and many other servants of God long after him, was the lunyoro translation of the 1662 *Book of Common Prayer* (*Ekitabu ekyokusaba kwa bantu bona*). This lunyoro or kihema prayer book was used in and around Boga as the Church expanded. But the use of this book in a language of Ugandan origin obliged people who were not of the same linguistic expression to learn this language as a language of the Church, since the liturgy, the songs, the administration of the sacraments and the catechism were written in kihema.

The liturgy in kihema (lunyoro) has been practiced in this way since the Anglican Church entered the Congo in 1894, until the creation of the first Congolese Diocese in 1972. This liturgy, which had a touch of both English and Hema culture, was practiced for a long time in a country with a great diversity of tribes. This book in Kihema is still in use in the Boga church and in other Hema-speaking parishes. As for the other parishes, they are currently benefiting from the translation of the *Prayer Book* into other national and international languages.

- 3.2. Translating liturgical books

When the Diocese of Mboga was created in 1972, the Church's expansion had already taken it far from the area of influence of the Lunyoro language. The new bishop, Philip Ridsdale, his wife and deaconess Lucy felt it necessary to translate the Lunyoro Book of Common Prayer into Swahili, one of the major national languages spoken throughout eastern Congo, Tanzania, Kenya and other neighbouring countries.

They began by translating the Morning *Prayer and Evening prayer* onto typewritten sheets. The first prayer book, *Kitabu cha Sala kwa Watu Wote* (Livre de la Prière Commune), came off the presses of the Catholic Church in Bunia in 1973, a year after the creation of the Diocese of Boga. This prayer book contained morning and evening prayers, Holy Communion, adult and infant baptism, catechism and confirmation. In 1979, the 1973 book was reprinted, with the addition of marriage, burial of adults and children, dispatch of catechists, occasional prayers and more.

This first prayer book was supported by another - *Kawaida y a Ibada*. Similar to the Lectionary, this book was used in the Congo to keep to the liturgical calendar. However, its use was short-lived. The Bahema (Banyamboga) seemed to have no interest in this new Swahili book, as they already had their own. Moreover, it should be pointed out that it was not the entire translation of the Book of Common Prayer that was made into Congolese Swahili. It was only a few extracts of the essential services as indicated above.

After its great expansion into eastern Congo from the 1970s onwards, the time had come for the Anglican Church to move out of the Swahili zone. So, in 1979, the little Swahili book was translated into Lingala, another national language spoken in Kinshasa and north-west Congo.

In 1980-1981, Mgr Ndahura Bezaleri, then Bishop of the Diocese of Bukavu and Archbishop of the Province of Rwanda, Burundi and Zaire, prepared another *Book of Common Prayer* in Swahili, this time using the Church of England's *Alternative Service Book* (1980) and the Episcopal Church of the USA's Book *of Common Prayer* in French (1979). At the same time, he ordered the translation of this work into Ciluba, another national language spoken in south-western Zaire (Congo), for the two Kasais that were part of the Diocese of Bukavu.

In 1984, the new Swahili book, still in extracts but already well structured, was printed by the *Society for Promoting Christian Knowledge* (SPCK) in London, under the supervision of Mgr Patrice Njojo Byankya. The latest revised translation of *Kitabu cha Sala* dates from 1998. It was seriously revised into good Swahili by Canon lan Terrant, a CMS/London missionary working in the Diocese of Aru, under the supervision of Mgr Patrice Njojo Byankya, Archbishop of PEAC and Bishop of the Diocese of Boga.

This book in Swahili contains almost all the services necessary for a good Anglican liturgy in all circumstances and occasions, the liturgical calendar, etc. It has nothing to envy other *Book of Common Prayer* in use within the Anglican Communion.

The translation of the Prayer Book into Ciluba, produced under the supervision of Mgr Dirokpa Balufuga Fidèle, Bishop of the Diocese of Bukavu, hit the presses of the Catholic Church of Kananga in 1985, with financial support from the Society for Promoting Christian Knowledge (SPCK/London). This great achievement in Ciluba was made possible thanks to the great help of the Venerable Mukendi Mpinga Casimir, Archdeacon of Kasaï Oriental and the Venerable Mubibwa, Archdeacon of Kasaï Occidental.

In addition to these prayer books in the three Congolese national languages and in Lunyoro, the Episcopal Church of the USA's *Book of Common Prayer* (1979/1983) is used for worship in secondary schools, in cathedrals sometimes or in town, at meetings of intellectual groups, in diocesan or provincial synods, during ecumenical or international meetings, on official days with the presence of state authorities, etc.

In addition to the above-mentioned prayer books, we should mention the use of prayer books in Kinyarwanda (in the territories of Masisi and Rutshuru) and in Kikiga (Bunganza, Kikumiriro...) in certain parishes bordering the Diocese of Bukavu with Rwanda and Uganda, especially for hymnology.

The Church of Mboga is often criticized for imposing Kihema on the neighboring population in the Anglican Church of Congo, but the same mistakes have also been made by Swahili-speakers in Eastern Congo, where the Swahili Prayer Book was imposed on tribes who didn't know the language. Examples include the Diocese of Aru, where Bangala (a version of Lingala) and several local languages are spoken, Mahagi, where Alur is spoken, and the territory of Masisi in the Diocese of Bukavu, where Kinyarwanda is spoken. Circumstances, however, have dictated that the prayer book be translated into these local languages, as initially there were no ministers of God available.

Among the liturgical books currently in use in the Anglican Church of Congo are the EAC prayer books in local, national and foreign languages.

The liturgical books in local or national languages used in the Anglican Church of Congo are :

- *Ekitabu ekyokusaba kwa Bantu bona* in lunyoro, used mainly in the Boga regions since the time of Apolo Kivebulaya. The most recent version of this book dates from 1961;
- *Kitabu cha sala kwa watu wote* in Swahili dated 1986. This book is used in the Dioceses of Aru, Boga, Bukavu, Kisangani, Kindu, Nord-Kivu and Katanga. It has been widely distributed after several editions (1973, 1984 and 1986);
- *Bukuyalosamboyabatobanso o   lingalaekosalelama   o eklezyaanglicane   o*
  Congo in Lingala (1979). It is used in the city-province of Kinshasa, in Central Congo, in the former provinces of Bandundu and Equateur, and in the western part of the new province of Tshopo. The diocese of Aru also has its own Prayer Book in Bangala (a kind of Lingala).
- *Mukanda wa masambila a Bantu bonso mu chiluba mudiwo mu ekleziaanklicane,* in Ciluba or Tshiluba (1985). This prayer book is used in the present-day provinces of Kasaï Oriental, Kasaï Central and Kasaï.

Liturgical books in foreign languages include :

In French, *the Book of Common Prayer* from the USA (1983) or Canada. This book is used in some EAC dioceses, which organize worship in French alongside worship in the national language, either on Sundays, at youth meetings, in the provincial synod, on national holidays with the presence of officials, etc.

In English, *The Book of Common Prayer* (1662), revised according to the country (Nigeria, Uganda or Kenya). This book is used in some dioceses alongside worship in the local language, notably in Kinshasa, where there is a large community of Nigerian origin, in Bukavu, etc.).

The multitude of books in a Diocese is not without its difficulties for the Bishop in administering the sacraments, and also for other ministers who do not share the same linguistic expression.

All in all, the *Book of Common Prayer* was used in the Congo only in Mboga in lunyoro. The Book of Common Prayer in its true sense has therefore never been translated by the Anglican Church of Congo until now. The prayer book in Swahili, Lingala and Chiluba consists only of extracts. Often, these are extracts from documents already translated by people who, in many cases, have not mastered the ineffable richness of the language into which they are translating. It's only natural, then, that the quality of the translation, as well as the substance of the document, should require serious revision for a good liturgy.

14.1 Birth and development of the Province of Burundi, Rwanda and Zaire (PBRZ)

The Archbishops of the Ecclesiastical Province of Burundi, Rwanda and Zaire

NDAHURA BEZARELI
Zaire, 1980 - 1981

NDANDALI Justin
Ruanda, 1982 - 1987

SINDAMUKA Samuel
Burundi, 1987 - 1992

In 1980, the countries forming the Francophone Council within the Church of Uganda, each with two Dioceses (Rwanda with the Dioceses of Kigali and Butare, Burundi with Buye and Bujumbura, and Zaire with Mboga-Zaire and Bukavu), the conditions required for the creation of an Ecclesiastical Province having been met, the Provincial Synod of the Church of Uganda authorized these three French-speaking countries of Central Africa to form their own French-speaking Ecclesiastical Province. These countries thus broke away from the Church of Uganda.

At the 1980 Francophone Council meeting in Bukavu, Bishop Ndahura Bezaleri of Bukavu was elected Archbishop of this new Francophone province. And on May 11, 1980, Africa's first French-speaking ecclesiastical province, the Province of the Anglican Church of Burundi, Rwanda and Zaire, was inaugurated. Archbishop Ndahura Bezaleri was enthroned as Archbishop of the new province by His Grace Robert Runcie, Archbishop of Canterbury (who had ordained him to the priesthood in 1974 at St. Alban's Cathedral, England) and His Grace Silvanus Wani, Archbishop of Uganda, Burundi, Rwanda and Zaire (Church of Uganda).

The provincial seat was thus established in the diocesan office of Bukavu, where the new Archbishop was Diocesan Bishop. The Archbishop's term of office was fixed at 5 years by the Constitution of the new Province, and the archiepiscopal see was rotational. This meant that no Archbishop, during his term of office, was allowed to build a provincial office in his own country. Instead, he had to use his diocesan office for provincial affairs.

On July 15, 1980, Dirokpa BalufUga Fidèle, an evangelist in training for the diaconate in Boga, was elected Provincial Secretary by the first Provincial Synod of the PBRZ, held in Bukavu. Dirokpa BalufUga Fidèle was not ordained a deacon until October 14, 1980 in Boga by the new Bishop of Mboga-Zaire, Mgr Njojo Byankya Patrice.

The inauguration of the new French-speaking province was followed by other happy events, including the consecration of other bishops and the opening of new dioceses within the province.

Despite their withdrawal from the English-speaking world, the churches of Rwanda, Burundi and Zaire were still struggling to carry out their mission effectively. It was difficult for them to take into account the specific characteristics of each country in terms, for example, of the Church's political involvement.

When His Grace Ndahura Bezaleri died on December 25, 1981 in Bukavu, he was replaced at the   head of the province by   a Rwandan subject   ,
Bishop   Justin Ndandali.
Butare, who was enthroned on June 6, 1982 at the Huye stadium in Butare (Rwanda). The provincial headquarters were moved to Butare, in accordance with the PRBZ provincial constitution. Its Provincial Secretary was the Reverend Canon André Kaizari.

Under the leadership of Mgr Justin Ndandali, the province has set up a provincial house in each of its member countries. Each year, the UTO (*United Thansgiving Offerings*), an organization of mothers of the Episcopal Church in the USA, grants subsidies to each province of the Anglican Communion, to be distributed to its dioceses for specific projects according to their requests.

It was in this context that His Grace Justin Ndandali requested and obtained from the College of Bishops that UTO subsidies be centralized for three years, at the level of the provincial office, with a view to purchasing a house to be used for income regeneration, for self-financing projects, in favor of the Anglican Church in each country. This was done. Zaire was the first beneficiary, enabling it to buy two provincial houses in Goma, in the Diocese of Bukavu. The second round went to Rwanda, with the purchase of a provincial house in Butare. Burundi had to wait for the third round. Its provincial house was bought in Bujumbura.

At the end of his mandate, His Grace Justin Ndandali was replaced by Samuel Sindamuka, Bishop of Bujumbura (Burundi). On June 9, 1987, he was enthroned as 3^e Archbishop of the PBRZ in Bujumbura. At the same time, the seat of the province was moved from Butare to Bujumbura. The Reverends Severin Ndayizeye and Pie Ntukamazina succeeded each other as provincial secretary.

Five years later, His Grace Samuel Sindamuka's term of office came to an end. The College of Bishops of the PBRZ, instead of repeating the 2^e round of rotation by country, saw fit to divide the Province into three, so that each country would become an autonomous ecclesiastical province in its own right.

In 1992, at a meeting of the College of Bishops of the BRZ French-speaking Province held in Bujumbura, it was decided to divide this Ecclesiastical Province into three, depending on the country, after 12 years of open cohabitation. This project met with the approval of all participants.

During the meeting, representatives from each country elected their Archbishop. Samuel Sindamuka, Bishop of Bujumbura, was elected on behalf of Burundi; Augustin Nshamihigo, Bishop of Shyra, on behalf of Rwanda; and Njojo Byankya Patrice, Bishop of Mboga-Zaire, on behalf of Zaire. The churches of Burundi and Rwanda chose other denominations. They became respectively Eglise Episcopale du Burundi (PEEB) and Eglise Episcopale du Rwanda (PEER); the Church of Zaire preferred to keep its denomination of Eglise Anglicane du Zaïre (CAZ).

The Province of the Church of Burundi, Rwanda and Boga-Zaire was thus split into three new Provinces , each of which became an Ecclesiastical Province. autonomous. The Anglican Province of Rwanda (*Eglise Episcopale du Rwanda*) was inaugurated on June 7, 1992, and its first Archbishop was His Grace Augustin Nshamihigo. The Province of the Anglican Church of Burundi *(Eglise Anglicane du Burundi)* was inaugurated in January 1992. Its first Archbishop was His Grace Samuel Sindamuka.

14.2. Evolution of the Province of the Anglican Church of Zaire (PEAZ)

The Archbishops of the Ecclesiastical Province of the Anglican Church of Congo

NJOJO KAHWA Patrice
1992 - 2002

DIROKPA BALUFUGA Fidèle
2003 - 2009

ISINGOMA KAHWA Henri
2009 - 2016

MASIMANGO KATANDA Zacharie
2016 -

On May 30, 1992, the autonomous Ecclesiastical Province of the Republic of Zaire, known as the Province of the Anglican Church of Zaire (PEAZ), was inaugurated in Bukavu. It comprises five dioceses: Zaire, Bukavu, Kisangani, Katanga and Nord-Kivu.

The date of May 30 is very significant in the history of the EAZ, as it commemorates the death of Apolo Kivebulaya, the pioneer of the EAZ. On the occasion of the inauguration, His Grace Njojo Byankya Patrice, Bishop of the Diocese of Boga, was enthroned as the first Archbishop of the EAZ. A few days later, on June 2, 1992, the 1er Provincial Synod elected Reverend Molanga Botola Jean, Provincial Secretary of PEAZ. The administrative and head office of PEAZ was set in Bunia.

The new Archbishop bought a large plot of land in Bunia and built a provincial office to house the various provincial departments, as well as a house to house the Provincial Secretary.

His Grace Patrice Njojo Byankya led the Anglican Church of Congo to its centenary in 1996 (1896-1996). In 2002, he reached the end of his second mandate after 10 years at the head of the PEAC.

On October 3, 2002 in Lweza (Kampala), Mgr Dr Dirokpa BalufUga Fidèle, Bishop of the Diocese of Bukavu, was elected Archbishop of the PEAC, to succeed His Grace Patrice, who will henceforth assume the functions of Diocesan Bishop of Boga, pending his retirement, in accordance with the Article of the Provincial Constitution.

Archbishop Dr Dirokpa Balufuga Fidèle was enthroned as the 2nd Archbishop of the Province of the Anglican Church of Congo on February 16, 2003, in Bukavu's Saint Peter's Cathedral.

Following this enthronement, on the following Sunday, February 23, 2003, His Grace Williams Rowan was enthroned as the 104e Archbishop of Canterbury. His Grace Dr Dirokpa B. Fidèle represented the PEAC as its Primate at this grandiose ceremony.

The fifth Provincial Synod, held from February 16 to 19, 2003 in Bukavu, decided to transfer PEAC's administrative and social headquarters from Bunia to Kinshasa and to create the Missionary Diocese of Kinshasa (as it did not yet meet the conditions for the creation of a classic Diocese). Bishop Dirokpa B. Fidèle was officially installed as Diocesan Bishop of Kinshasa on December 20, 2003, in accordance with the Provincial Constitution of the PEAC.

The reasons behind the creation of the new Diocese of Kinshasa and the transfer of the PEAC headquarters to the capital of the DRC are as follows: Firstly, to extend the Gospel to the West of the country, as the EAZ had, until now, concentrated its evangelization efforts in the East of the Country. Secondly, to have permanent contacts with the political and religious authorities and other development organizations, all based in Kinshasa, for the well-being of the Church and the Congolese population in general. Finally, to have a legal and valid representation of the Anglican Church of Congo in the capital and to possess the necessary infrastructure for the visibility of the Church.

As soon as he arrived in Kinshasa, the new Archbishop's main concern was to focus on evangelization and to provide the PEAC with the basic material infrastructure and buildings it needed to function properly. Thus :

- On July 2, 2004, a bishopric was purchased in Limete/Kinshasa, which also serves as the Archbishop's residence (because it's the same person). This 4-acre building was sold in 2008, to buy another 8-acre building in "Masina Sans Fil", in a more spacious, attractive and comfortable plot for a bishopric or archbishopric;
- As mentioned above, construction began on a building measuring 18m by 12m. In 2005, the foundation stone was laid for a 2-storey building to house the provincial and diocesan offices, with the first floor serving as a chapel and multi-purpose hall. The building was completed on May 17, 2009. It is located on avenue Basalakala no. 11, at the junction with avenue de l'Université;
- A former 39-room lut hotel was also purchased in 2006 from Mikondo/Kimbanseke, to serve as a church, school, health center and home for the pastor and other church staff;
- Six other empty plots were also purchased for other projects. of the Church, in the future at Badara II, commune of Kimbanseke.

The various departments were also organized: the Provincial Secretariat, Evangelism, Theological Formation and Sunday School, *Mothers'* Union, Youth, Community Development Office and Medical Service.

However, given the country's economic and social situation, it was not possible to operate all provincial departments in Kinshasa. As a result, some departments continued to operate in the interior of the country: Medical Service, in Béni (North Kivu) with Albert Baliesima Kudikima, Community Development Service, in Bukavu (South Kivu) with Fidèle Mushamuka, Youth in Bunia (Province Orientale, now Ituri province) with Miss Judy Acheson, the presidency of the Mothers' Union in Kindu (Maniema) with president Maman Naomi Amunazo Katanda, in Kindu (Maniema) and secretary Maman Damali Sabiti in Bunia (Province Orientale), not forgetting the PEAC Liaison

Office with M. Frédéric Ngadjole, who provided a great service to all the PEAC Dioceses at the Liaison Office in Kampala. All these departments functioned harmoniously thanks to modern communication technology, the Internet.

His Grace Dirokpa Balufuga Fidèle was replaced by Mgr ISINGOMA KAHWA, Bishop of Boga, at the head of the PEAC. He was enthroned on August 09, 2009, by His Grace Dirokpa Balufuga F., as the 3ᵉ Archbishop of the PEAC, in Kinshasa (Salle de conférence du jardin Botanique de Kinshasa). As such, he replaced His Grace Dirokpa as Bishop of the Diocese of Kinshasa.

On April 12, 2013, Venerable Antonio KIBWELA, was appointed Provincial Secretary of the PEAC, replacing Bishop Molanga Botola Jean, appointed Missionary Bishop for the EAC, in the Republic of Congo- Brazzaville, on November 07, 2012.

His Grace Isingoma Kahwa Henri, was re-elected, by the College of Bishops, meeting in Butembo, in April 2014, for the 2ᵉ 5-year term, at the head of the PEAC.

This 2ᵉ mandate was due to expire in 2018, but His Grace Isingoma has meanwhile *resigned,* from his position as Archbishop of the Province of the Anglican Church of Congo and ipso facto, from that of Bishop of the Diocese of Kinshasa, during the 8ᵉ National Synod of the EAC held in Bunia/Mwito, in February 2016, the reason given being that of health.

Enthronement of the 4ᵉ Archbishop of the Anglican Church of Congo (2016 -)

The College of Bishops of the EAC, meeting under the chairmanship of the Dean of the Province, Mgr FUNGA Lambert, Bishop of the Diocese of Kisangani, from July 10 to 13, 2016, at the Catholic Parish of St. Elois, Beau Marche/Kinshasa, unanimously elected, on July 11, 2016, Mgr MASIMANGO KATANDA Zacharie, Bishop of the Diocese of Kisangani. Elois, de Beau Marche/Kinshasa, unanimously elected, on July 11, 2016, Mgr MASIMANGO KATANDA Zacharie, Bishop of the Diocese of Kindu, as the Archbishop of the EAC, replacing His Grace Isingoma Kahwa Henri, who resigned.

His enthronement took place on September 11, 2016, at Saint Peter's Anglican Cathedral in Kinshasa, during the Eucharistic celebration, which had been well attended by Anglican faithful from the diocese of Kinshasa and others from the inland dioceses of the Ecclesiastical Province of the EAC, to which should be added Christians of other religious denominations. There was also a strong delegation of visitors from the worldwide Anglican Communion. These included: Personal representative of the Archbishop of Canterbury, Mgr...

According to the spirit of the amended EAC Constitution of February 2016, the new Archbishop will have his National Office in Kinshasa, but will reside in his diocese of origin, where he remains the titular Bishop. While the Provincial Secretary, with permanent residence in Kinshasa, will manage the day-to-day affairs of the Church in regular contact with the Archbishop.

Today, the Ecclesiastical Province of the Anglican Church of the Congo comprises twelve dioceses, one of which is missionary, that of the Republic of Congo/Brazzaville (12). The first five dioceses were created between 1972 and 1996, i.e. before the EAC Centenary (1996): Boga, Bukavu, Kisangani, Katanga (Shaba) and Nord-Kivu. The 7 other new dioceses were created between 1997 and 2016, namely the dioceses of : Kindu, Kinshasa, Aru, Kasaï, Kamango, Goma and Congo/Brazzaville. There are twelve diocesan bishops, one of whom is also Archbishop, and one assistant bishop, for the time being: Mgr Elisha Tendwa (Tanzanian), assistant bishop of the Katanga diocese, based in Kalemie.

It should be noted that the expressions "Province de l'Eglise Anglicane du Congo" and "Eglise Anglicane du Congo" express the same reality (PEAC = EAC), since, for the moment, there is only one Anglican ecclesiastical Province in the DRC (7). However, the Constitution of the said Province authorizes its splitting into two or more new ecclesiastical provinces, on the decision of the Provincial Synod, when the need arises. For the moment, the last National Synod held in Bunia, in February 2016, maintained the single appellation: "L'EGLISE ANGLICANE DU CONGO" [EAC], instead of the Province de l'Eglise Anglicane du Congo [PEAC].

14.3. Provincial Departments

14.3.1. Provincial Department of Evangelization

The Provincial (or National) Department of Evangelization was created in February 1995, at a meeting of the Provincial Executive Committee held in Bunia, under the chairmanship of His Grace Archbishop Njojo Biankya. On that occasion, the first national coordinator of this Department was elected in the person of Venerable Ise-Somo of North Kivu, who beat the other candidates in the running: Canon Musubaho of Boga, Venerable Bahati of Bukavu and Venerable Mavatikwa of Kisangani with 16 votes out of 23.

This department has a number of achievements to its credit, notably in the fields of evangelism and training.

On the subject of evangelization, let's cite a few examples:
- Evangelism and food assistance to displaced persons in Ituri (war between Hema and Lendu) and to displaced persons in Kanyabayonga, Kirumba and Rutshuru;
- The organization of evangelization campaigns in the various Dioceses;
- The financing of the reconciliation meeting in the Diocese of North Kivu in 2003 for a total amount of 3620$;
- Prison evangelism;
- Evangelism among the military in North Kivu, South Kivu, Maniema and Ituri. 16342 soldiers heard the Gospel, 8723 received Jesus Christ as Savior and Lord, this happened between the years 2008 and 2009.

On the subject of training, please note :
- The organization of evangelization seminars in the various Dioceses;
- Seminars for school chaplains ;
- The search for scholarships and the training of evangelists from different dioceses for the CCLK in Goma;
- *Langham Preaching*'s training of local preachers and facilitators in the various Dioceses ;
- Equipping participants with evangelism books and Bibles.

On the subject of church planting, note:
- Several contributions for the construction of   chapels and   schools in the region some Dioceses ;
- The purchase of land for the church in Lubero in the Diocese of North Kivu;
- The purchase of a concession for the church in Yumbi, Bandundu in the Diocese of Kinshasa;
- Purchase of a plot of land in Boma, Bas-Congo for the church (Diocese of Kinshasa).

14.3.2. Provincial Medical Department

The medical service of the Province of the Anglican Church of Congo began with an infirmary whose main task was vaccination. It was located at the entrance to the Mboga Anglican Church.

Over the years, the Anglican Medical Service has evolved, gradually expanding into the various Dioceses of the DRC, thanks to the leadership and vision of the late Dr Patricia Nickson, the late Miss Nyangoma Kabarole, Dr Nigel Pearson, Mr Albert Baliesima and many others.

The activities of the medical service (SM PEAC) have been integrated into the   DRC's health system   since   1984   with the   creation   of the   first   health   zone   managed   by   the SM in Boga. Two new health zones have recently been opened, in Kamango (in North Kivu) and Mahagi (in the current Ituri province), under the management of SM PEAC.

Through its medical department, PEAC currently manages 59 health centers, 3 hospitals, 5 medical centers, 2 modern dentistries and 45 health posts.

The medical department has 3 areas of intervention: health in general (management of health centers, rehabilitation, water and sanitation services), HIV/AIDS and sexual violence, and emergencies.

14.3.3. The Provincial Department of Jeunesse Chrétienne Agape en mission(JCA)

We can't talk about the Youth Department without mentioning Miss Judy Acheson, who spent her entire missionary life in the DRC mentoring the youth not only of the Anglican Church of Congo, but

Congolese youth in general. She was a British missionary sent by the Church Mission Society, since 1980 working with the Anglican Church of Congo. She is a graduate of the Institut Superieur Pedagogique in England. She began her ministry among children in Ituri, in the diocese of Boga. In 1989, she opened the Youth Department in the same diocese, with the aim of training young people to assume their responsibilities for the glory of God. Seeing the great change in the lives of these young people, in 1996 the Bishops asked her to take charge of the youth of the DRC.

She was thus appointed National Coordinator of the "AGAPE" Christian Youth Mission based in Lubumbashi.

ThisDepartmentbeganinLubumbashieninAugust1988whereitwascalled "Vijana vya Maji ya Uzima" (VMU). In February 1989, it was launched in Bunia under the name "AGAPE".

JCA's mission is to provide a framework for all children, teenagers and adults, without discrimination as to religion, sex or social rank, with a view to empowering them and enabling them to take responsibility for their own future and the future of the nation.

JCA pursues the following objectives:
- Welcoming and supporting all young people without discrimination;
- Introduce children to their rights and their place in the family, the Church and society. society to obtain justice and recognition of their inalienable dignity;
- Leading young people to discover and accept Christ for themselves ;
- Introduce young people to the Gospel of Christ through a variety of activities;
- Raising awareness of certain problems in life that are likely to arise in the future their harmonious development and, consequently, that of society;
- Stimulate young people to take charge of their future and that of the nation;
- Make young people aware of the importance of their role both in the development of the Church, society and the nation;
- Helping each   young person to find appropriate solutions   for his or her   own   needs economic and social problems through the exercise of his talents, intellectual qualities, spiritual, moral and physical abilities;
- Encourage young people to participate in theological and scientific training with a view to foster their vocation for the well-being of the Church and the nation.

Given the importance of these young people and their commitment to God's ministry, the Church decided to incorporate them into the PEAC on May 31, 1996, during the third ordinary session of the Provincial Synod, which coincided with the celebration of the centenary of the Anglican Church of Congo in 1996. Gradually, this Department was opened in each Diocese of the PEAC in 2001. For the sake of uniformity, it was called "Jeunesse Chrétienne Agape", or JCA for short.

On October 18, 2006, the Bishops added "on mission" to the name of this group of young Anglicans, to signify the mission it is charged with fulfilling.

Currently, three towns are home to JCAM's coordination services and managers ???? The coordinator, Reverend Bisoke Balikenga, and the secretary, Mr Ucama, are based in Bunia. Vice-coordinator Jean-Bosco Chishweka and treasurer Mr Lumbala Micky live and work in Lubumbashi. Reverend Azama Adolphine, in charge of the girls' section, lives in Kindu, Maniema. Despite this dispersal, all these JCA coordinators work together and everything is progressing normally, by the grace of God.

As part of its philosophy, the JCA organizes the following activities to attract young people:
- *The Boys and Girls Brigade and Scouting*: in the history of the Anglican Church, we find movements created by two Anglican friends: Alexander Smith, who started with the *Boys Brigade*, and Baden-Powell with Scouting. The brigade has much more discipline with parades, but both movements have a program that contains many activities with the same objectives of bringing young people to Christ. The brigade operates in the Diocese of Katanga and scouting in the Diocese of Bukavu.
- *Choirs*: JCA en mission sees music as a strategy for spreading the Christian faith around

the world. The activities of choirs and/or orchestras are therefore considered to be of paramount importance within the youth group. Using their talents, choir members compose and publish songs for praise, worship and civic, moral and Christian education.

- *Ecolededimanche* : leDépartementdela jeunessemarquéqueques
children in the DRC are marginalized. They don't go to school, and are abused as slaves by adults, and even by their parents, who send them out onto the streets or throw them out because they are declared, rightly or wrongly, to be witches. These children have no vision of the future, no hope of living. JCA, on a mission, realizes that these children are deprived of their rights, and takes it upon itself to support them through a section at their service at the PEAC.

This JCA section supervises children in :
- Training parents, making them aware of their responsibilities and responsibilities ;
- Sharing Bible stories and other activities with children;
- Introducing them to the service of Christ.
- *La trompette troupe*. It is organized by the JCA en mission of the Diocese of Kinshasa. The troupe is well known for its films and its practical teaching and advice for young people. In its first film, entitled "Jeune, fais tout mais..." (Young, do everything but...), the trumpet establishes clear links between its lessons and those of our first manual, entitled "Réjouis-toi dans ta jeunesse" (Rejoice in your youth). Evangelist Jean- Marie Ntumba is the initiator and writer of all these productions, whose actors come from several churches. Unfortunately, the troupe is not currently operating, following the departure of its initiator from the Anglican Church.

Among the activity centers organized by JCA are :
- Bunia youth center. It acts as a center for activities, meetings and hospitality;
- The Makabo agricultural center in Bunia. It was responsible for raising awareness and training agricultural groups in rural areas (this center no longer exists ????).
- The Tumaini center for traumatized girls and girl mothers in Bunia. This center (no longer in existence ????) looked after girls who had been raped or traumatized by the massacres and looting of their families during the war, as well as those living with HIV/AIDS. The center detraumatizes them and teaches them to read and write, sew and knit, live in a group and value themselves in society.
- The voluntary screening center for sexually transmitted diseases (HIV/AIDS, sexually transmitted infections, etc.) in Bunia, which works in partnership with the PEAC medical service.

JCA also organizes various sessions for young people, including :
- Fighting HIV/AIDS in partnership with the PEAC medical service;
- Leadership training for young people;
- Changing mentalities and a sense of responsibility;
- Detraumatization in wartime environments;
- Peace and reconciliation, especially in Ituri, for the benefit of tribes divided by conflict. war.

Center de Formation des Encadreurs des Jeunes in Mahagi.

We can't conclude our analysis of the Youth Department without mentioning the Centre de Formation des Encadreurs des Jeunes (CFEJ in French) in Mahagi.

Located in the city of Mahagi, in the territory of the same name, in the present-day province of Ituri, this center was created in 2004 by Miss Judy Acheson. Its objectives are to:
- Providing students with theoretical and practical knowledge in youth management;
- Helping students design programs to meet their needs and expectations
aspirations of the young people they have to supervise, in relation to the realities of their environment;
- Introduce students to the ways in which young people can gain

experience

with Jesus Christ ;

- Introduce students to the importance of correctly identifying the major problems facing young people, and helping them to find their own solutions.

Since August 2004, the center has welcomed young leaders from all over the DRC, Uganda and South Sudan for specialized training in youth ministry. Leadership, child and youth psychology, youth and society, development and spirituality are the main subjects taught at the center.

In addition to training youth supervisors, the CFEJ's Board of Directors decided to create the *Institut Supérieur des Techniques d'Animation Sociale* (ISTAS) in 2008. This higher education institution, also located in Mahagi, offers two courses of study: social animation and management information systems.

Here is the list of General Managers who have worked at the Centre AGAPE in Mahagi:

- . Reverend William Bahemuka Mugenyi, from 2004 - 2011
- . Venerable Jean-Marie Kithoko Kabange, from 2011 - 2013
- . Reverend Martin Nguba, from 2013 -

14.3.4. Development and Social Works Department

HISTORY AND EVOLUTION OF THE DEVELOPMENT AND SOCIAL WORKS DEPARTMENT OF THE ANGLICAN CHURCH OF CONGO (EAC): 19802016

This history is presented in the form of Table 2 in the Appendix to this work. The table in question is a summary of the social works carried out by the Church under the aegis of its various pastors. We have limited ourselves to summarizing the achievements implemented through the efforts, lobbying and advocacy of the EAC national office. It is important to note, however, that in each EAC Diocese, several development actions have been initiated and carried out for the socio-economic and health well-being of the communities. These include schools, health centers, vocational training centers, the prevention of and fight against SGBV, peace and reconciliation between communities in conflict, environmental management and agro-pastoral activities,

PROVINCIAL PRESIDENTS OF THE UNION DES MERES

KAMANYOHA NJOJO
1992 - 2002

MARIE RII KAHORO DIROKPA
2003 - 2004

GODELIVE MUGISA ISINGOMA
2009 - 2016

NAOMIE AMUNAZO KATANDA
2004 - 2009
2016 -

DAMALIE SABITI
1992 - 2009

JOSEPHINE MASUKA
2009 - 2016

VIRA MAMBOYABO MARTHE
2016 -

The *Mothers'* Union is a women's organization that brings together women from the various dioceses and ecclesiastical provinces of the Anglican Communion. Its mission is evangelism and other family and socio-economic activities.

The organization was founded in England in 1876 by a mother named Elisabeth Mary Sumner. She was born into a family of three children, of whom she was the youngest. It was a family with a good Christian testimony, who loved God and were totally devoted to His service.

A brief history of the Mothers' Union department

In 1992, at the enthronement of the I^e Archbishop of the new ecclesiastical province of the Anglican Church of Congo in Bunia, His Grace Njojo Byankia Patrice, the College of Bishops of the PEAC appointed coordinators for the various departments. The Mothers' Union department was headed by Maman sa Grâce Kamanyoha Njojo as President and Madame Damalie Sabiti as Provincial Secretary of the Mothers' Union.

Some of our achievements

Under their responsibility, they had set up the office in Bunia where they worked in collaboration with other departments such as BDC, ETE, Evangelization...

- Meetings of bishops' wives and diocesan secretaries were held in Kampala.
- Christian development and education training ;
- Drafting of the statutes and internal regulations of the mothers' union;
- Setting objectives, values, mission and vision
    1. **Objectives:**
    - Promoting and supporting married life
    - Encouraging parents in their role of developing their children's faith
    - Maintaining a worldwide fellowship of Christians united in prayer, worship and service
    - Promote favourable conditions in society for a stable family life and the protection of children
    - Helping people whose family life is experiencing adversity.
    2. **Values**: L'union des mères is firmly rooted in a voluntary ethic.
       Its governance, leadership and programs are driven by members and realized by the world, as they respond to God's call to faith and action.
    3. **Beliefs :**
       - We believe in the value and equality of each individual;
       - We believe in the value of relationships: Jesus said "You shall love the Lord your God with all your heart and with all your soul and with all your mind." and love your neighbor as yourself.
       - We believe in the value of the family in all its forms as a source of love and support for individuals and the foundation of a caring community.
    4. **Vision**: is that of a world where God's love is manifested through relationships of love, respect and so on.
    5. **Mission:** To demonstrate the Christian faith in action by transforming communities around the world through nurturing the family in all its forms.

In 2003, His Grace Dirokpa Balufuga Fidèleet was elected Archbishop of the EAC, and his wife, the late Mama Marie Rii Kahoro, became Provincial President of the Union des Meres, continuing to work with Mama Damalie Sabiti as Provincial Secretary of the UM.

When President Mama Her Grace Marie RII KAHORO Dirokpa passed away in 2004, the College of Bishops decided that the wife of the Bishop of Kindu, Mama Naomi Amunazo Katanda, should continue in her role as President of the Mothers' Union, working alongside Secretary Madame DamalieSabiti.

In 2009, His Grace Dirokpa BalufUga Fidèle retired and Mgr Isingoma Kahwa Henri was elected Archbishop, and his wife Maman Godelive Mugisa Isingoma took over the presidency of the provincial Mothers' Union, with Maman Joséphine Masuka as secretary.

During this period, the vision of development and the launch of the millennium objectives in the fight against poverty and the promotion of women in the consolidation of peace in the world; the union of mothers had generated a structure called UFPPS, which *stands for "Union des Femmes pour la Paix et la Promotion Sociale"* (*Union of Women for Peace and Social Promotion*); whose aim is to promote, value and encourage women to be messengers of peace and to participate in integral development.

The UFPPS has a vision of women's well-being, without distinction of denomination; it works with all religious denominations.

In collaboration with our country DRC, as part of the fight against sexual violence against women, UFPPS has been financed by the European Union, DIFD and Tearfund to fight against gender-based sexual violence in Eastern DRC. In favor of survivors of violence, the following activities have been carried out:

- Training religious leaders on sexual violence and IGA management
- Learning trades according to the needs of each group;
- School education for children born of rape;
- Purchase of rehabilitation equipment;
- Revenue-generating activities (RGA)
- Microcredit

With the help of the Mothers' Union, the beneficiaries were well served and well looked after through this 1UFPPS structure; and the others had accepted Jesus as their Savior and remained in the Church to serve God in our community.

As part of the promotion of women and the fight against illiteracy, the Union des mères provinciale had trained diocesan secretaries in practical literacy with the support of Mary Sumner House, training trainers who in turn trained other trainers in their respective dioceses.

Mothers and daughter-mothers were the direct beneficiaries, having testified that they knew how to read the Bible.

In 2007, the ENP [Ensemble Nous Pouvons] approach reinforced the philosophy of self-care in dioceses where this approach was applied, such as the diocese of North Kivu, Boga and Aru. The other dioceses are still in the experimental phase. This approach has helped and continues to help the Churches in the field of development and church planting, and the mothers who are members of the Mothers' Union are pioneers in this approach.

In 2016, SagrâceIsingoma took early retirement and in the same year , the The college of bishops elected Monsignor Masimango Katanda Zacharie and his wife Maman Naomi Amunazo Katanda as president of the provincial and national Mothers' Union as agreed, and by a vote of the bishops, Maman Vira Mamboyabo Marthe was elected National Secretary and coordinator of the Mothers' Union department.

The Mother's Union central office is located in London, England, in a building called Mary Sumner House. This office supervises and pays the salaries of the Mother's Union *Work* Secretaries, as well as ensuring their travel within their Diocese or Province. At the level of the Ecclesiastical Province, there is a Provincial Secretary whose salary is paid by the central office, as well as travel within the country and abroad on official business.

The provincial office also organizes capacity-building training both within the country and abroad, especially for the exchange of experience.

15. THE CENTENARY OF THE ANGLICAN CHURCH OF ZAIRE (1896-1996)

All in all, it was in the last two decades of its centenary that the Anglican Church experienced extraordinary expansion. The history of the Anglican Church of Zaire over its hundred years of existence recalls above all the difficulties of its establishment. The Church suffered not only from the discriminatory policies of colonialists and missionaries, but also from the aggressive fervor of certain local Protestant communities and the doctrinal problems arising from the hasty acceptance of members of marginalized churches during its geographical growth.

Despite the various obstacles and shortages it has suffered, its evangelizing achievements are countless, thanks to the courage and determination of Apolo Kivebulaya's ministry.

In fact, since Apolo's first visit, the Anglican Church of Zaire has continued to spread throughout the country. In the space of a hundred years, it has spread from Mboga to the eastern part of the Congo, and then to the center and west of the country, all the way to the Atlantic Ocean. Starting with a small group of Apolo converts, the Anglican Church has baptized more than half a million faithful over the past hundred years in five dioceses with a total of over 300 parishes and 32 archdeaconries.

All in all, the Anglican Church of Zaire reached an important milestone in 1972, with the creation of its first Diocese, that of Mboga-Zaire. Another crucial step was the inauguration of the Province of the Anglican Church of Zaire (PEAZ) on May 30, 1992. By becoming a Province, an autonomous administrative structure was created within the worldwide Anglican Communion.

Since 1960, the Congolese-run Anglican Church of Congo has been present in the 11 administrative provinces, prior to the territorial division of January 2016.

One of its main priorities has been theological education. That's why it has created many Bible schools, including the Institut Supérieur de Théologie Anglican (ISThA) in Bunia, which offers university-level teaching. Many other students have been trained in other theological or university institutions at home and abroad. Its major concern is to equip the Church with intellectual leaders, capable of solving the problems posed by contemporary society: exercising a holistic ministry, participating in high-level theological debates, inculturating the Gospel and the liturgy, and so on.

We remain convinced that, beyond the balance sheet, the establishment of a Church without a local cultural dimension cannot contribute to the effective rooting of the Gospel. In this case, the Gospel is like a layer of varnish on a traditional cultural backdrop, constantly resurfacing when Christianity fails to satisfy, because it remains alien or indifferent to the practical situation on the ground.

On the occasion of the centenary, thousands of devotees from all corners of the globe gathered in Boga on May 30, 1996 to pay homage to the works of Apolo Kivebulaya, thank God for his dedication and celebrate his work and teaching. Their admiration was overwhelming, as evidenced by the exclamation of Bishop Bruce Stavert, Anglican Bishop of Quebec (Canada), who was present at the ceremonies: "What a tribute this is to Apolo, and a measure of faithfulness to the Lord on the part of his disciples" (9).

The Anglican Church is alive and kicking throughout the Congo, despite its material poverty and the difficulties it has survived.

Today, it's unlikely that any other obstacles will stand in the way of its activities. In one hundred years, the progress made is notorious thanks to the concerted efforts of natives, partners and missionaries, especially from CMS/England, Australia and Ireland, Mid-Africa Ministry, the Episcopal Church in the USA and Canada, and so on. They all deserve our gratitude for their sacrifices and dedication to the cause of the Gospel. Of course, there is still much to be done in many areas where their contributions continue to be indispensable.

May the centenary of the Anglican Church of Congo be the occasion to take stock of the spiritual, physical and material health of the Church, with a view to ensuring its harmonious development and that of its members in particular, and of the Congolese population in general, in the years following the centenary.

NOTES

Second Era A.

(1) Bezaleri Ndahura, *Implantation de l'Église anglicane au Zaïre,* Mémoire de licence, unpublished, Faculté Protestante de Théologie, Kinshasa, 1974, p.99.

(2) Yossa Way, *La Spiritualité de l'Eglise anglicane du Congo face aux défis contemporains,* Thèse de doctorat en théologie, unpublished, Université protestante du Congo, Kinshasa, 2009, p.82.

(3) Dirokpa BalufUga, *La liturgie anglicane et l'inculturation hier, aujourd'hui et demain : regard sur la célébration eucharistique en République Démocratique duCongo,* Thèse de doctorat en théologie, unpublished, Université Laval, Québec-City, Canada, 2001, p.36.

(4) Canon Bill Norman, in *Centenary of the Anglican Church in Zaire*, p.23.

(5) Ridsdale Lucy and Philip, *Note on Bishop Dirokpa's letter 6.11.1998.*

(6) ISTHA, *A Brief History of the Anglican Church in Zaire*, 1996, p.9.

(7)Tim Naish, *An Experience of Francophone Anglicans*, in Andrew Wingate, *Anglicanism a Global Communion*, Kevin Ward and Carrie Pemberton (Ed.), Nowbray, 1998, p. 165.

(8) Yossa Way, *op.cit.* ,p. 122.

(9) Mgr Bruce Stavert, in *Centenary of the Anglican Church in Zaire*, p.25.

Part 4
Second period of 2ᵉ Period
Chapter 4

B. THE INFLUENCE OF EVANGELICAL WORKS AFTER THE CENTENARY (1996-2016)

1. Political change in the country and its impact on the churches

On May 17, 1997, Mzee Laurent Désiré Kabila's AFDL (Alliance des Forces pour la Libération du congo-Zaïre) forces entered Kinshasa and won a crushing victory over the forces and regime of Joseph Désiré Mobutu Sese Seko, then President of the Republic of Zaire. Following this change of regime, the country changed its name back to the Democratic Republic of Congo (DRC), as it had been called before October 27, 1971.

The Anglican Church of Zaire is renamed: Eglise Anglicane du Congo (EAC), and the Ecclesiastical Province of Zaire: La Province de l'Eglise Anglicane du Congo (PEAC). Churches are free to continue using old Christian names of foreign origin at baptisms. Evangelization resumes its normal course, despite material and financial difficulties.

The so-called AFDL war of liberation, led by Rwandan, Ugandan and Congolese soldiers, also known as Kadogo (Petits soldats or child soldiers, or children associated with armed forces and groups) began in Uvira in November 1996. After crossing the Congo from east to west, they triumphantly entered Kinshasa on May 17, 1997. This caused President Mobutu to flee to Gbadolite, then to exile in Togo and Morocco, where he died.

At the end of the AFDL war, on July 27, 2008, President Laurent-Désiré Kabila demanded the departure of the Rwandan and Ugandan soldiers who had lent him a hand, but who were behaving like potentates in the country. These rebels organized an offensive on Goma and Bukavu, which they easily overran on August 2, 2008. They then landed by plane in Moanda (Bas-Congo) with a view to attacking the city of Kinshasa and ousting the new president from power. But they were driven out of Bas-Congo and Kinshasa by Mzee Kabila's army, supported by the Angolan and Zimbabwean armies.

The Rwandan soldiers of the RCD and their Congolese accomplices then retreated into the interior of the country. Over time, and with the emergence of other rebel movements, the Congo would eventually be crumbled into five parts ruled by autonomous local rebel governments: Azarias Ruberwa Manywa's RCD in Goma, Mbusa-Nyamwisi's Rassemblement Congolais pour la Démocratie Kisangani Mouvement de Libération (RCD/K-ML), Roger Lumbala's Rassemblement Congolais pour la Démocratie National (RCD/N) in BaiWasende, Jean-Pierre Bemba Gombo's Mouvement de Libération du Congo (MLC) and Joseph Désiré Kabila Mzee's Gouvernement légal in Kinshasa. Each movement has its own president, governmental team, autonomous armed force and administration.

These troubles came to an end at the Dialogue entre Congolais after several meetings under the aegis of international mediators in Lusaka, Gaborone, Addis Ababa, Pretoria and finally *Sun City*, South Africa in 2002. There, under the mediation of Senegal's Moustapha Niasse, the Congolese agreed to the formation of a 1+4 Government, comprising a President of the Republic and 4 Vice-Presidents, who formed a Transitional Government for a five-year period (2002-2006).

All these wars and their consequences have not failed to destabilize the Anglican Church, as indeed all other Churches: large numbers of refugees to deal with, loss of life, destruction of Church infrastructures and the environment, and so on.

Another tribal war, just as atrocious as the first two, broke out in Ituri and struck at the very heart of the Anglican Church from 2001 to 2003. It caused countless material and human losses.

2. Installation of the Anglican Church of Congo liaison office in Kampala

The Anglican Church of Congo's liaison office in Kampala, Uganda, set up in 1997 by decision of the College of Bishops, was created on foreign soil following the almost total breakdown of communications systems (post offices, banks, radio stations, etc.) in the Democratic Republic of

Congo, as a result of the recurring wars of liberation mentioned above.

The primary purpose of creating the liaison office was to serve as a bridge between the local church in the DRC and the outside world during the period when the country was almost suffocated by the effects of war. This objective has remained unchanged to this day, although there has been a marked improvement in communications. However, stability and security remain fragile and precarious in eastern Congo.

From 1997 to June 2002, this office was run respectively by Miss Pat Clay, a missionary from the Church Missionary Society (CMS) in England, assigned to the Diocese of Boga, and Miss Margaret Crewes, commonly known as "Maggie", an Australian missionary in the Diocese of North Kivu (CMSA), both in refuge in Kampala/ Uganda.

From July 2002 to the present day, the office has been managed by Mr. Frederick Ngadjole, a Congolese missionary assigned to Uganda.

It is important to note, by the way, that this liaison office is not a Department of the Province of the Anglican Church of Congo. Rather, it is a special missionary technical unit, attached to the provincial office for a clearly defined renewable mandate with a very precise objective. It is a point of reference for both the outside world and the natives. The current operating contract runs until the end of December 2017.

Since its creation, the office has benefited from the financial support of *Trinity Church Wall Street* in the United States and the *Church Missionary Society* in England.

This office is located within the Anglican Church of Uganda administrative complex at the following physical address: "Willis Road, Namirembe Hill, Mothers' Union Building/Namirembe Diocese, Upper Floor".

The liaison office plays the following roles:
- Receive and guide both leaders and members of the Anglican Church of Congo than partners on a service mission in Uganda or just passing through;
- Help them regularize their travel documents, if necessary;
- Manage the post office box "25586 Kampala, Uganda" for the benefit of the Province of the Anglican Church of Congo and its members;
- Facilitate financial transactions for the benefit of PEAC, when necessary;
- Channel all correspondence to its destination;
- To provide the necessary orientation information to people wishing to contact the Anglican Church of Congo on various levels;
- To act as a link in bilateral transactions between the Anglican Church of Congo, its Departments, institutions and the outside world, when necessary;
- Carrying the banner of the Anglican Church of Congo in Uganda, up to a certain limit;
- Carry out any other task assigned by the hierarchy , within the limits of its authority . competence.

N.B. The liaison office of the Anglican Church of Congo plays a very important role in the life of this community, for without its presence, the functioning of our Dioceses would become impossible.

3. The creation of new Dioceses within the PEAC
3.1. Diocese of Kindu

Peter Dawson
Ass Bukavu à Kindu
1992 -1997

MASIMAGO KATANDA Zacharie
1997 -

The Anglican Church was established in Maniema, precisely in Kindu, in 1972 through the *"Eglise Protestante Libre du Congo"* sect. This Protestant sect, which had not been granted civil status, joined the Anglican Church when the Zairian government decided that all Protestant churches should be members of the Church of Christ in Congo (ECZ), as mentioned above.

Mgr Peter Dawson, CMSA, was consecrated Assistant Bishop of the Diocese of Bukavu on February 2, 1992 at Saint Andrew's Cathedral, Sydney, New South Wales, by His Grace Donald Robinson, Archbishop and Bishop of the Diocese of Sydney, Australia. He was sent to Kindu in 1992 to prepare the new Diocese of Kindu.

August 30, 1997 saw the inauguration of the 6e Diocese of the PEAC: Diocèse de Kindu with the consecration and enthronement of Mgr Masimango Katanda Zacharie in Kindu, by His Grace Patrice Njojo Byankya, Archbishop of the PEAC. He was thus the first bishop of this new diocese, which resulted from the split of the Diocese of Bukavu.

Maman Naomi Amunazo Katanda was the first President of the Mothers' Union of the Diocese of Kindu. From 2004 to 2009, she was also Provincial President of the Mothers' Union, replacing Maman Marie Rii Kahoro Dirokpa, who died in 2004.

3.2. Diocese of Kinshasa

MAVATIKWA KANY
Ass. Kisangani à Kinshasa
1997 - 1999

DIROKPA BALUFUGA Fidèle
2003 -2009

ISINGOMA KAHWA Henri
2009 - 2016

Achille S. MUTSHINDU MAYAMBA
2016 -

Anglicanism was introduced to Kinshasa by American Anglican missionaries working for international organizations. The first Anglican community in Kinshasa was established by the Reverend Theodore Lewis in 1967   .
assigned as an official of the International Development Agency (A.I.D.) in Kinshasa. As an Anglican priest, he looked after a small English-speaking Anglican community in Kinshasa, under the supervision of the Archbishop of Zambia.

In 1974, the Reverend Ndahura Bezaleri, legal representative of the Anglican Community of Zaire in Mboga, travelled to London via Kinshasa. In Kinshasa, he met pastors and catechists who claimed to be Anglicans and who had already opened four parishes, in Livulu (led by Lumbala), Bumbu (administered by Mavatikwa), Makala (led by Mario) and Ndjili (governed by Kabengele).

Back in Mboga, Ndahura Bezaleri reported to his bishop, Philip Ridsdale, who sent the Reverend Beni Bataaga   , then a   diocesan   development officer, as
in charge of the Anglican Community of Kinshasa in 1979.
When he arrived, his first task was to teach people about Anglicanism: liturgy, sacraments, accounting, church administration, etc. He was also involved in the development of the Church of England.
Secondly, he was busy looking for plots of land: he bought a plot of land in Livulu with funds from Mgr. Ridsdale; then a large house in Limete quartier Funa as residence and Anglican center of Kinshasa with money from Tearfund; he built a Church in Ngaliema, the money coming from the contribution of servants of God and parishioners; he had the purchase and construction of a Church in Bumbu with Christians' own funds and this construction was completed by Mgr. Isingoma in 2001.
In Makala and Selembao, Christians rented places of worship from non-Anglicans,
He had also initiated worship in English for diplomats from the British Embassy, the United States of America, Liberia, etc.
He also started French worship in Kintambo in the building of a Baptist church. He sent the leaders of these churches from Kinshasa to Boga to be trained and ordained priests. The others were sent to Kisangani to be trained as catechists.
Apart from these church activities, he was looking for settlement visas for Anglican missionaries.
Here are the people who supported him when he arrived:
- Dr. Lobo Iwa Djugudjugu and especially his wife Mariam Kabadjungu
- Diplomats of Great Britain, the United States of America and Liberia
- Dieudonne Tambaki family
- Isingoma Constatin family
- André Rwaheru family
- Mrs Indy Bijwerenda and others.

He left Kinshasa in November 1989 for the diocese of Mboga and was replaced by Venerable François Bolamba, sent by the diocese of Kisangani.
Later in 1997, the Venerable Mavatikwa Kany, Archdeacon of Kisangani, was consecrated Bishop and sent to Kinshasa as Assistant Bishop, but sadly died just as he began his episcopal ministry in Kinshasa on December 29, 1999.

Following the death of Mgr Mavatikwa Kany, Assistant Bishop of the Diocese of Kisangani, with residence in Kinshasa, Mgr Henri Isingoma Kahwa, Bishop of the Diocese of Katanga, in exile at the time, was dispatched in 2000 by the College of Bishops of the PEAC to Kinshasa to administer this Archdeaconry and continue the preparation of the Diocese of Kinshasa, a task previously devolved to the late Mgr Mavatikwa.

The Anglican Church is more concentrated in the eastern part of DR Congo. Right from the start of evangelization, in 1896, the Church's administrative headquarters were established in Mboga. It was not until 1992, the year of the enthronement of the first Archbishop and the creation of the Ecclesiastical Province, that it was transferred to Bunia (120 km north-east of Boga). Despite the creation of the Ecclesiastical Province of the Anglican Church of Congo, it was not until 2003 that a diocese was opened in the west of the country, notably in Kinshasa, the country's capital.

In 2003, the Provincial Synod of the Anglican Church of Congo, held in February 2003 in

Bukavu, decided to transfer the Anglican Church's headquarters to Kinshasa in order to strengthen its activities in the western part of the Democratic Republic of Congo and in Congo Brazzaville. In fact, according to the constitution of the Province of the Anglican Church of Congo, the Archbishop of the said Province is ex officio Bishop of the Diocese of Kinshasa.

So, on December 20 , 2003, at the official inauguration of the 7ᵉ Diocèsedela PEAC: the Diocese of Kinshasa, with the installation, at the Cathédrale du Centenaire Protestant de Kinshasa, of His Grace Dr Fidèle Dirokpa Balufuga, formerly Bishop of the Diocese of Bukavu, as the first Bishop of this Diocese. This Diocese was born of the division of the Diocese of Kisangani.

His Grace Fidèle Dirokpa will continue to serve at the same time as Titular Bishop of the Diocese of Bukavu until 2006, when the new Bishop of this Diocese, Bishop Sylvestre Bahati Bali-Busane, will be enthroned. During the ceremony, the Reverend Jean Molanga Botola, Provincial Secretary of the PEAC, was consecrated by His Grace Fidèle DirokpaBalufuga , Assistant Bishop of the Diocese of Kinshasa at the Cathedral of Bukavu.

Protestant Centenary in Kinshasa.

The first concern of the new Archbishop and Bishop of the Diocese of Kinshasa, as soon as he moved in, was to provide the new Diocese, which housed the Provincial Office, with a dignified infrastructure for the harmonious operation of its two institutions, the diocese and the province. In fact, there was only one dwelling house, purchased at the time of Bishop Henri Isingoma Kahwa. This house served as a home for the Provincial Secretary's family, for the Bishop of the Diocese of Kinshasa, for the diocesan and provincial offices, and as a chapel for Sunday worship. Working conditions were far from efficient at the start of diocesan and provincial activities in Kinshasa.

On July 2, 2004, with the help of UTO (USA), Jersey Deanary (UK) and Congo Church Association (CCA), a house was purchased for the residence of the Bishop of the Diocese of Kinshasa, who is also the Archbishop of the PEAC according to the PEAC Constitution.

On March 14, 2005, Apolo Kivebulaya's death dream, "Bury me with my head to the west, so that the Lord's work may continue", was fulfilled.

The Diocese of Kinshasa had sent the first evangelist, Hilaire Wasoga, to establish the Anglican Church of Congo in Moanda/Banana, at the mouth of the Congo River, 109 years after Ugandan evangelists had introduced Anglicanism in Mboga. It should be noted that Hilaire Wasoga is a former Christian from the Diocese of Kindu, who worked for an oil company, SOCIR, in Moanda, and who gladly accepted this position. In 2009, this fledgling church was visited by the Bishop of the Diocese of Kinshasa, Miss Judy Acheson, in charge of Youth, and Maman Rosalie Etsa, Secretary of the Union of Mothers of the Diocese of Kinshasa.

On May 15, 2005, the groundbreaking ceremony took place for the construction of a 2-storey building (12 m x 18 m) to house provincial and diocesan offices on the first floor, as well as serving as a church and multi-purpose hall. The building was completed on May 17, 2009. But the ground floor had already been in use as a chapel and multi-purpose hall since July 2007, as had some of the first-floor rooms as offices. All that remained was a few finishing touches.

Other unoccupied houses and plots were also purchased, to house other diocesan and provincial services.

On August 9, 2009, Mgr Henri Isingoma Kahwa, then Bishop of the Diocese of Boga, was enthroned by His Grace Fidèle Dirokpa BalufUga, as the 3ᵉ Archbishop of the PEAC in Kinshasa in the Salle de Conférence of the Botanical Garden of Kinshasa. On the same date, His Grace Dr Fidèle Dirokpa Balufuga, having reached the constitutional age of retirement, went to rest, after 30 years of effective and full ministry, in honor of God (1979 -2009).

On June 13, 2010, a large community of Nigerian Anglicans, living in Kinshasa, discovered the Anglican Church of Congo and joined the Cathedral Parish of Saint Peter in the Diocese of Kinshasa .

Anglican Cathedral in Kinshasa, support for other chapels and parishes, the purchase of a vehicle for the Church, the purchase of land from the Commune of Ngiri-Ngiri for the construction of the

Anglican Cathedral of Kinshasa and other noteworthy one-off services, etc.

On November 7, 2012, Mgr Jean Molanga Botola, Provincial Secretary and Assistant Bishop of the Diocese of Kinshasa, was appointed Missionary Bishop for the EAC of the Republic of Congo-Brazzaville. He was replaced as Provincial Secretary by Venerable Antonio Kibwela on April 12, 2013.

On January 31, 2016, Bishop Achille Sébastien Mutshindu Mayamba was consecrated in Kamango, by His Grace Henri Isingoma Kahwa, as Assistant Bishop of the Diocese of Kinshasa. His consecration took place at the same time as that of Mgr Daniel Sabiti Tibafa, Bishop of the new Diocese of Kamango, in the north-east of the DRC.

Mgr Achille Sébastien Mutshindu Mayamba, was elected titular Bishop of the Diocese of Kinshasa on July 12, 2016, by the EAC College of Bishops, meeting in c- extraordinary session in Kinshasa from July 10 to 13, 2016. In this capacity, he replaces His Grace Isingoma Kahwa Henri, who was also Bishop of the Diocese of Kinshasa, but who resigned in February 2016 for health reasons, according to his statement.

Mgr Achille Sébastien Mutshindu was enthroned on September 11, 2016 at Saint Pierre Cathedral in Kinshasa, as the 3e Titular Bishop of the Diocese of Kinshasa by His Grace Masimango Katanda Zacharie, himself enthroned on the same date, as 4e Archbishop of the Anglican Church of Congo.

Anglicanism reached the Aru and Mahagi region through the Congo Lai Anglicans from Uganda. The Mahagi Anglicans, having learned that there was an Anglican diocese in Boga, asked for Anglicanism to be implanted there, as they were experiencing an identity crisis within the CECA-20, which does not admit infant baptism, for example.

The Bishop of the Diocese of Boga, Philip Ridsdale, responded favorably to their request, and the Anglican Church in Mahagi was opened on December 24, 1979, while in Aru it was opened on March 13, 1982. It should be noted that all those involved in the establishment of Anglicanism in Aru and Mahagi were lay people.

The 8e Diocese of the PEAC was inaugurated on November 13, 2005 with the consecration and enthronement of Bishop Georges Titre Ande as its first Bishop by His Grace Fidèle Dirokpa BalufUga. This Diocese is the result of the split of the Diocese of Boga.

Located in the former Province Orientale, in the far north-east of the DRC, on the border with Uganda, the Diocese of Aru is essentially made up of two administrative territories: Aru and Mahagi.

3.4. Diocese of Kasai

MARCEL KAPINGA
2010 -

OLAHOYE ABIODUN & THERESA
2005 -2008

The inauguration of the 9ᵉᵐᵉ Diocese of the PEAC, known as the Diocese of Kasai, took place on January 30, 2011 with the enthronement of Mgr Marcel Kapinga Kayibabu at the Stade Tshikisha in Mbuji-Mayi (Kasaï-Oriental), under the presidency of the Dean of the Province , Mgr Zacharie Masimango Katanda, Bishop of the Diocese of Kindu, assisted by the Assistant Bishop of the Diocese of Kinshasa and the Provincial Secretary of the PEAC, Mgr Jean Molanga Botola. This Diocese comes from the division of the Diocese of Kinshasa, after 28 years of preparation by its Diocese of origin, that of Bukavu.

The consecration ceremony of Bishop Marcel Kapinga took place in Butembo on December 12, 2010, together with Bishop Ise-Somo, 2ᵉ of the Diocese of North Kivu.

As we have said, in its origins, the Anglican Church in the two Kasais was formed by members of the sects known as "Balondi Ba Yesu", a group of sects each with its own doctrine, but occasionally praying together.

In 1977, following the State's suppression of certain sects with no civil personality, the "Balondi Ba Yesu" sent one of their number, the former Honoré Kaseya Tshidinda, to Boga, the historic seat of the Anglican Church in the DRC, then Zaire, to seek legal documents for recognition and integration.

Papa Honoré Kaseya obtained all the necessary documents from the Venerable Festo Byakisaka Bomera, then Deputy Legal Representative of the Anglican Church. The elder Kaseya thus became the first leader of the Anglican Church in Kasaï Oriental, while in Kasaï Occidental, Kalala Dipa Dia Nzambi was appointed.

In 1980, Mgr Ndahura Bezaleri, the 1ᵉʳ Bishop of the Diocese of Bukavu, on which the two Kasais depended, came on a pastoral visit. At that time, Kasai Oriental was ruled by the former Kanyinda Lusangu and Kasai Occidental by Mudibua Tshiongo Wa Minanga.

With a view to equipping these two Churches with true Anglican doctrine, it was decided to send candidate servants of God to study for their formation: Kasaï Oriental sent Julien Ciakudia Kaseya and Casimir Mukendi Mpinga, while Kasaï Occidental sent Mudibua Tshiongo Wa Minanga and Mukendi Mukoma. They were ordained deacons in 1982 in Bukavu and returned to their respective provinces, except for Julien Ciakudia, whom Bishop Ndahura had sent to Canada for university theology studies.

In 1985, the two Provinces became two separate Archdeaconries. Kasaï Oriental, under the direction of Vénérable Casimir Mukendi Mpinga, and Kasaï Occidental, under the administration of Vénérable Mudibua Tshiongo, who died in 1998.

From 1998 to 2001, following the death of the Venerable Mudibua, the leadership of the church was entrusted to a College made up of the Reverends Kabasele Mudibua, Bandowe Shimba Yabo and Kabeya Ngoyi. This collegial administration was headed by Kabeya Ngoyi, who was interim Archdeacon from 2001 to 2003.

From that year onwards, Reverend Kabeya Ngoyi was appointed Archdeacon by Bishop Dirokpa Balufuga of the Diocese of Bukavu. He continues to head the Kananga Archdeaconry.

In 1987, Casimir Mukendi Mpinga was confirmed Archdeacon of the Archdiaconate of Kasaï Oriental. In 1996, the Archdeaconry of Mbuji-Mayi gave birth to the Archdeaconry of Kabinda, headed by the Venerable Ngoyi Lubilaji.

From 1977 to 2005, the Anglican Church of the two Kasais depended on the Diocese of Bukavu, i.e. for 28 years. In 2005, the Diocesan Synod of Bukavutenu decided to place the two Kasais under the jurisdiction of the new Diocese of Kinshasa, under the direct control of His Grace Fidèle Dirokpa Balufuga , who had already taken the first steps with the Diocese of Kinshasa. preparing the future Diocese of Kasaï.

Back in 2004, Bishop Dirokpa Balufuga met a retired missionary, the Reverend Stuart Broughton and his wife Cathryn, in Jersey (British Isles). He had interested them in the great preparation of the new Diocese of Kasaï and the need for the permanent presence of a missionary in this field of evangelization.

This couple didn't hesitate for a moment to volunteer for this mission. They will come as missionaries with their   personal salaries   ,   but under the cover   of the CMS/England for added credibility. The couple were based in Mbuji-Mayi and worked in both Kasai for two years. In carrying out their mission, the emphasis was on biblical teaching and training for the holy ministry. It was this couple who bought the current Bishopric of Mbuji-Mayi.

After the departure of this missionary couple, the Bishop of the Diocese of Kinshasa asked CMS/England to send a new missionary to continue the preparation of this new Diocese. The head of CMS (Diana Witts) replied that her organization had no missionaries to send to the DRC at that time. Instead, she advised us to contact CMS Nigeria. We then contacted His Grace Peter Jaspar Akinola, the Archbishop Primate of all Nigeria. This request was quickly granted, and a Nigerian missionary with the necessary skills and knowledge of French was found in the person of the Reverend OLAOYE Abiodun and his wife Theresa. He was consecrated bishop on October 14, 2005 at Christ Church Cathedral, Marina, Lagos, Nigeria, by the Primate of the Province of the Anglican Church of Nigeria, His Grace Peter Jasper Akinola. The ceremonies were attended by the Bishop of Kinshasa and other delegates from Kinshasa.

He was sent to the DRC as a missionary and Assistant Bishop of the Diocese of Kinshasa, with residence in Mbuji-May, where he arrived on November 22, 2005. Accompanied by his wife Theresa, they took charge of spiritual and moral preparation, as well as self-financing development projects. They gave renewed hope to the future of the Diocese.

With the arrival of this man of God in November 2005, the administrative structure of the Church was able to evolve rapidly. From 3 archdeaconries, it grew to 9, including 5 in Kasaï Oriental and 4 in Kasaï Occidental.

During the three years they spent in Kasai, this missionary couple did a great deal of work: seminars, refresher courses and conferences were held for servants of God and lay Christians, office equipment and a vehicle were purchased, and evangelization campaigns were organized.

From then on, the Church of Kasaï felt ready to receive its Diocese, although certain conditions had not yet been fulfilled. At the Provincial Synod held in Kinshasa from February 10 to 17, 2008, it was decided that the Diocese of Kasai would be inaugurated in November 2008. The first elections were held in May 2008. But due to internal conflicts and leadership struggles, they were cancelled and reorganized in October 2008.

From these elections, the Venerable Marcel Kapinga Kayibabu was elected 1[er] Diocesan Bishop for the two Kasais, which were ratified by the College of Bishops at its meeting in Bunia on April 1[er] 2010.

Ordained to the holy ministry in 1998, Marcel Kapinga Kayibabu was appointed interim Dean and Archdeacon of Kabinda in 2003. He became confirmed Archdeacon in 2007, replacing Venerable Ngoyi, who died in 2006.

History being the study of past events, it would be ungrateful to end this point without mentioning Honoré Kaseya Tshidinda, Léonard Kazadi Muana and Donatien Kanyinda Lusangu, these great figures whose contribution was decisive in the establishment and evolution of the Anglican Church of Kasaï. Of course, in addition to these great figures, other people have, through their self-sacrifice and dedication, evangelized not only Kasaï Oriental but also Kasaï Occidental and the city of Kinshasa Province (e.g. Honore Kaseya et al.).

For this diocese to evolve serenely, its pastors and followers must banish all the scourges that plague them, and agree to look in the same direction, working on the following three axes of the vision of fulfillment: evangelization, development, teaching and training.

The first Diocesan Synod was held from July 21 to 24, 2011. It had three key items on the agenda: the review and adoption of the Diocesan Constitution; the development and adoption of the action plan; and the design, development and adoption of the Diocesan operating budget.

SABITI TIBAFA Daniel
2016 -

In Apolo Kivebulaya's day, Kamango was already a chapel. The chapel evolved and became an Anglican parish in 1956.

The Diocese of Kamango is the tenth of the Anglican Church of the Congo. It was inaugurated on January 31, 2016 with the consecration and enthronement of Bishop Daniel Sabiti Tibafa, by His Grace Isingoma Kahwa Henri, as its 1er Diocesan Bishop. This Diocese originates from the split of the Diocese of Nord-Kivu.

On the same date of January 31, 2016, in Kamango, another bishop was consecrated, Bishop Achille Sébastien Mutshindu, who will be Assistant Bishop of the Diocese of Kinshasa.

MUKANIRWA KADORHO Désiré
2016 -

1.6.   Diocese of Goma.

The new Diocese of Goma comes from the split of the Diocese of Bukavu. The extraordinary elective Synod of this diocese held in Bukavu, from July 28 to 29, 2016, had elected 2 candidates. The Diocesan Synod of the Diocese of Bukavu had thus selected 2 bishop-candidates to present to the College of Bishops, for choice by election, namely: Reverend Désiré Mukanirwa Kadorho, with 51 and Reverend Birizeni, with 50 votes.

The College of Bishops, in its meeting of September 12, 2016, held in Kinshasa, had elected Reverend Désiré Mukanirwa Kadorho, as the 1e Bishop of the new diocese of Goma. His coronation and enthronement will take place on November 20, 2016, in Goma.

1.7.   Missionary diocese of Congo/Brazzaville.

The Anglican Church of the Republic of Congo, one of the Archdeaconries of the Diocese of Kinshasa, was granted on November 07, 2012, a Missionary Assistant Bishop, in the person of Bishop Molanga Botola Jean, formerly the Provincial Secretary of the PEAC and Assistant Bishop of the Diocese of Kinshasa. This Archdiaconate will continue to operate under the supervision of the Diocese of Kinshasa.

The EAC National Synod held in Bunia/Mwito in February 2016 conferred on the Archdeaconry of Congo/Brazzaville the status of an autonomous missionary diocese. Mgr Molanga Botola Jean, fat confirmed as Missionary Bishop for this new autonomous diocese, whose inauguration date will soon be set, by the EAC College of Bishops. /

4. The Anglican Church in the Republic of Congo

In 1997, the Anglican Church was officially established in the Republic of Congo by the Venerable Banzouzi. However, since 1995, Mr. Bansimba and Raymond Banzouzi, then evangelists, had already introduced the Anglican Church to Brazzaville. As soon as he arrived in Brazzaville, the Venerable Banzouzi joined his twin brother, Mr. David Bansimba, and over 180 others from north and south Brazzaville. The Anglican Church thus began its activities in Brazzaville, in Bansimba's plot on Rue Ngambini n°11, in the Ngambio district of Mfilou-Brazzaville.

The Anglican Church of Brazzaville received its operating permit from the Ministry of the Interior, Security and Territorial Administration on December 20, 1998 under N°208/MiSAT/DGAT/DOR/SAG, after submitting its declaration in which the Church's objectives were clearly defined. This document was granted by the   Ministry because Mr .   Bansimba

had   built   an office for the   Church   on   his land,
which showed the Congolese state authorities that the Anglican Church was serious about having a fixed address in Brazzaville.

The Anglican Church was strengthened by the massive arrival of Rwandan refugees from North and South Kivu. These refugees had fled Rwanda in 1994, following the atrocity triggered by the death of the President of Rwanda, Juvénal Habyarimana, and had taken refuge in the various localities of Kivu (Goma and Bukavu). In 1996, when the refugee camps were dispersed by the Rwandan Patriotic Army (RPA), assisted by Congolese rebel soldiers, many refugees took the road to Kisangani, fleeing from this ruthless army. Some arrived in Congo Brazzaville in 1997, and in other neighboring countries such as Gabon, Cameroon and the Central African Republic.

Many of these refugees were Anglicans. They found refuge in Brazzaville and throughout the Republic of Congo. As a result, the Anglican Church is becoming a living, mature church in the interior of the country, where several parishes are now open.

In 1997, the Anglican Church underwent a considerable expansion with the presence of Rwandan Anglican refugees, who were initially based in Kintélé, 25 km from Brazzaville. At the time, Brazzaville was one of the archdeaconries of the Diocese of Kisangani.

In 1999, the Venerable Banzouzi succeeded in recovering the Christians of the South who had been scattered following the war between President Pascal Lissouba and his predecessor Denis Sassou Nguesso. In 2000, they found another place to pray in the Quartier Bwetambongo in Moungali, and in the course of that year, Mgr Isingoma, who had travelled to Brazzaville in search of a visa, met one of the Rwandans, by the name of Silas Munyaneza, currently one of the priests at the Beach. On another trip to Brazzaville, Bishop Isingoma confirmed three people in the Moungali chapel under the name of Christ the King.

In 2003, Mgr Funga, accompanied by the Venerable Eisa, visited Brazzaville and confirmed more than 10 people in Kintélé. In Brazzaville-centre, the Church was established in Latsieme at that time. In the meantime, the Archdeaconry of Kinshasa, on which the Anglican Church of Congo-Brazzaville depended, had itself become an autonomous diocese through the division of the Diocese of Kisangani. Its 1er Bishop was Mgr Fidèle Dirokpa BalufUga, who was also Archbishop of the PEAC.

Following the inauguration of the Diocese of Kinshasa on December 20, 2003, the Archdeaconry of Brazzaville had now become an administrative entity under the leadership of this new Diocese. In early 2004, Bishop Dirokpa visited the Church in Congo-Brazzaville with Bishop Molanga, Assistant Bishop of Kinshasa, and Venerable Mvunzi, Archdeacon of Kinshasa. The general observation was that in the archdeaconry of Brazzaville, there was a serious problem of division between the archdeacon and the Christians of his entity, especially with the Rwandan Christians, due to poor leadership impregnated with xenophobia.

The first diocesan synod, held in Kinshasa from March 21 to 28, 2004, decided to appoint another leader to head this archdeaconry. Canon Joseph Mabanza Ndaku (former Archdeacon of Matadi) was appointed Archdeacon of Brazzaville, replacing Venerable Raymond Banzouzi.

His first task was to reconcile the two communities, Rwandan and Congolese, whose cohabitation had become difficult due to poor leadership. He had to establish a climate of understanding and peace in the Church, to ensure its smooth running. He was then to take charge of teaching to build up the faith of the faithful and the training of candidates for the ministry.

In 2006, the Diocese of Kinshasa sent Reverend Mabaku to Brazzaville, to assist the local Archdeacon in the training of candidates for the diaconate. Unfortunately, none of these candidates were Congolese from Brazzaville.

The first ordination in Congo-Brazzaville took place on September 7, 2006. At this ceremony, the following five people were ordained deacons by Mgr Fidèle Dirokpa Balufuga, Bishop of the Diocese of Kinshasa. They were Félicien Musabyimana, Joas Kanyampeta, Vincent de Paul Havugimana, François Nkundineza and Boniface Mugemangango. They were all ordained priests on November 25, 2008 in Brazzaville by Mgr Jean Molanga Botola, Assistant Bishop of the Diocese of Kinshasa.

In August 2009, the Diocese of Kinshasa changed its bishop, following the retirement of Mgr

Fidèle Dirokpa BalufUga on August 9, 2009. He was replaced by Mgr Henri Isingoma Kahwa, now Archbishop of the PEAC and, ipso facto, Bishop of the Diocese of Kinshasa.

The ordination to the diaconate and priesthood, on the same day, of the first Brazzavillois Congolese, in the person of Reverend Nimbi Emmanuel, took place on July 08, 2012 at
Brazzaville by Mgr Isingoma, at the Palais du Congrès in Brazzaville. The Archbishop was accompanied by his Assistant Bishop, Mgr Jean Molanga, Canon Daniel Sabiti, the Rector of UAC/Bunia, Venerable Kithoko, the Director General of ISTAS/Mahagi at the invitation of the ordination candidate, a finalist from ISThA/Bunia.

As for   Reverend Silas Munyaneza   , he was ordained   deacon   on   April 12, 2015   ,   at the
Paroisse Saint Félix de Brazzaville by His Grace Henri Isingoma Kahwa.

To our great regret, death snatched Venerable Joseph Mabanza Ndaku, this valiant pastor, from our affection on October 4, 2012 in Kinshasa.

Following the death of Venerable Mabanza, the Diocesan Council of Kinshasa, under the presidency of Bishop Isingoma, made new appointments in the Church of Congo-Brazzaville. Thus, Bishop Jean Molanga Botola, Assistant Bishop of the Diocese of Kinshasa, was appointed Missionary Bishop for Congo-Brazzaville on November 7, 2012. The Reverend Félicien Musabyimana was appointed Archdeacon of the EAC of Congo - Brazzaville, dated December 5, 2012. His installation took place on April 27, 2014 in the garden of the Palais de Congrès in Brazzaville by Mgr Jean Molanga Botola, in the presence of a strong delegation from the Diocese of Kinshasa, including Honorary Archbishop Fidèle Dirokpa Balufuga.

5. University training for Anglican theologians
5.1.   In the graduai
The EAC trained theology graduates in its Institut Supérieur Théologique Anglican (ISTHA), created by His Grace Ndahura Bezaleri in 1981 in Bukavu and then transferred to Bunia in 1987, where it still operates today. Over the same period, other Congolese Anglicans have obtained the same graduation diploma in other Instituts Supérieurs de Théologie, in the Republic of Zaire and elsewhere.

5.2.   Licence level
The Reverend Ndahura Bezaleri was the first Anglican Congolese to graduate in theology in July 1974 from the Faculté Protestante du Congo in Kinshasa, after 78 years of Anglican church planting in the Congo. His thesis was entitled: *Implantation de l'Église anglicane au Zaïre*.

After Ndahura Bezaleri's licentiate, the EAC sent students to various institutions of higher and university education in the country and abroad, with a view to continuing their university studies; the majority left for the theological training that the EAC so urgently needed for the effectiveness of its ministry. At present, every diocese in the EAC has a number of theologians at graduate or licentiate level.

But there are 2 important reasons for continuing to train theologians at graduate and undergraduate level:a) to raise the level of God's cadres/servants so that the Church has an increasingly qualified staff as the population in general becomes better educated. The Church must not be left behind. We need graduates and licensees who will serve in all areas of the Church. b) We need ongoing training for graduates and licensees, as there will always be a certain number who will leave the service due to illness, retirement, a change of career, etc.

5.3.   Mastery level
At present, the EAC has three categories of Master's degree: the first category concerns the Master's degree obtained at the Faculté Evangélique de Bangui (FATEB), whose first laureates were Mgr Henri Isingoma Kahwa (in 1988), Reverend Martin Nguba in 1992 and Reverend Etienne Mbusa Bangau, in 1993. After these laureates, many other students defended their master's theses at FATEB, which, in its system, does not recognize the bachelor's degree cycle. After graduating, students go straight into the 3-year master's cycle. Under the Congolese equivalence system, this diploma is considered a licence.

The second category of master's degrees is those obtained at higher institutes and universities in the Congo or elsewhere, and which lead to a doctorate.

The third type of master's degree is the DEA (Diplôme d'Etudes Approfondies). The EAC currently has 3 executives trained to MPh and MTh level: Mgr Daniel Sabiti Tibafa, who obtained an MPhil (Master's in Philosophy) in theology from the University of Birmingham, England, in 2004; and the Venerable Christophe Kangamina Sabiti, who has a DEA (Diplôme d'Etudes Approfondies) in theology, from Shalom University in Bunia, DRC, in 2016. And the Reverend Mbusa Bangau, who obtained an Mphil from the Oxford Centre for Mission in 2012.

### 5.4.	Doctorate level

The Anglican Church of Congo produced its first Doctor of Theology in 2001, after 105 years of Anglican Church presence in Congo. The EAC currently has 4 Congolese Anglican Doctors of Theology. They are :

- Bishop Fidèle Dirokpa Balufuga , the first English-speaking Congolese to earn a diploma
  D. in theology from Laval University, Canada, on April 20, 2001.
  His thesis is entitled: *La liturgie anglicane et l'inculturation hier, aujourd'hui et demain: regard sur la célébration eucharistique en République Démocratique du Congo.* Doctoral thesis in theology, Université Laval, Québec-City, Canada, 2001.
- Mgr Titre AndeGeorges , was the 2e CongoleseAnglican to obtain a doctorate in theology.
  theology at the University of Birmingham in England in 2003.
  The title of his thesis: *Authority in the Anglican Church of Congo: The influence of Political Models of Authority and the Potential of "Life-Community", Ecclesiology for Good Governance,* Birmingham, University of Birmingham, 2003.
- The 3e doctorate in theology group graduated in 2012, from the Université Protestante du Congo (UPC) in Kinshasa:
    - Venerable Yossa Way, whose thesis is entitled *La Spiritualité de l'Eglise anglicane du Congo face aux défis contemporains,* Doctoral thesis in theology, Faculté Protestante du Congo, UPC, Kinshasa, 2012.
    - Reverend Kahwa Njojo, whose thesis is entitled: *Jesus and non-violence dans les évangiles synoptiques: Etude exégétique de Mt 5,38-48; Mc 11,15-17 ; Lc 23,34,* Thèse de doctorat en théologie, Kinshasa, UPC, 2012.

Copies of all these theses can be found on the Internet, in the UAC library in Bunia and in the libraries of the universities that awarded these diplomas, or elsewhere.

### 6.	Creation of the Anglican University of Congo (UAC)

The Anglican Church of the Congo, with a number of its licentiates and doctors, has seen fit to transform the Institut Supérieur Théologique Anglican (ISThA) into the Université Anglicane du Congo (UAC), comprising other faculties in addition to theology.

The Anglican University of Congo (UAC) was created in Bunia in 2010. It organizes the two university cycles and awards the bachelor's degree.

Indeed, after 29 years of existence of the Institut Supérieur de Théologie Anglicane (ISThA), dedicated to the training of executives in theology at graduate level, the leaders of this institution had the vision to train executives in other fields as well. Thus, in 2010, the Board of Directors, chaired by His Grace Henri isingoma Kahwa, decided to create the Anglican University of Congo with new Faculties that did not exist in the area.

Here are the Faculties organized by the UAC with the reasons for their choice:

1) The aim of the Faculty of Civil Engineering is to meet the construction needs of the new Ituri Province, by providing it with well-qualified engineers.
2) The Faculty of Mining and Geology, which aims to produce engineers capable of prospecting and exploiting the region's mineral wealth.
3) The Faculty of Psychology and Educational Sciences, whose aim is to train specialists in school administration.

4) The Faculty of Development, through which the University has made it its duty to train Development Technicians to help our communities develop using environmental resources.

5) The Faculty of Theology, formerly ISThA, which continues to train for the holy ministry, this time under the title of UAC, up to degree level.

6) The Faculty of Oil and Gas, whose aim is to train engineers who will be able to participate in the exploitation of oil from Lake Albert (Ituri), or even that of the Virunga Park in Kivu, and methane gas from Lake Kivu.

The Institut Supérieur Panafricain de Santé Communautaire (ISPASC), which previously operated independently in Bunia, has been annexed to the Université Anglicane du Congo (UAC) as a Faculty.ItsDirector, Mr. AmudaBaba, hasbeenappointedGeneralSecretary. Académique de l'UAC in February 2016.

In July 2016, Mr. Amuda Baba was appointed Rector of UAC by the EAC College of Bishops, held in Kinshasa from July 10 to 13, 2016. He replaced the Venerable Dr. Yossa Way, who had been acting Rector since the academic year 20152016.

UAC's first Management Committee, headed by Reverend Canon Daniel Sabiti Tibafa, the university's first Rector, was responsible for submitting the application for authorization to operate to the Minister of Higher and University Education (ESU), who approved the request, signing Arrêté NO 911/MINESU/CABMIN/MML/PK/2011 of May 11, 2001, renaming the Institut Supérieur Théologique Anglican (ISThA) the Université Anglicane du Congo (U AC).

The following is a list of successive General Directors and Rectors of the Institut Supérieur Théologique Anglican (ISThA) and the Université Anglicane du Congo (UAC) (1981-2010).

No	NAME and Post Name	Period	Duration	Observation
01	NDAHURA Bezaleri	1980-1981	1 year	Bukavu
02	Dr. William BAILLY	1981-1984	3 years	Bukavu
03	Jeremy Pemberton	1987-1988	1 year	Bunia
04	Susan Braoddus	1989-1990	1 year	Bunia
05	Isingoma KAWA Henri	1990-1996	5 years	Bunia
06	Peter Wood	1996-1999	3 years	Bunia
07	Title Ande Georges	1999-2000	1 year	Bunia
08	Buyana Mulungula	2000-2001	1 year	Bunia
09	Tite Ande Georges	2001-2007	6 years	Aru
10	Sabiti Tibafa Daniel	2007 to present	9-years	Bunia
11	Dr. Yossa Way interim	2015-2016	1 year	Bunia
12	Mr.Amuda Baba	2016		Bunia

In addition to the UAC, there are two other Anglican universities in the Diocese of North Kivu: the Université Anglicane Apolo Kivebulaya (UAAKi) in Butembo and the Université Anglicane en Afrique Centrale (UNAAC) in Beni, as well as the ISTM in Aru and the ISTAS in Mahagi.

7. The Anglican Church of Congo in international debates on Anglicanism

The Anglican Church of the Congo, now equipped with high-level executives, confidently takes part in the burning debates of the day within the worldwide Anglican Communion, on which its fate also depends. Concrete action to defend and conquer the Anglican identity within a large, predominantly English-speaking communion began in 1985. The reunion will take place through various meetings, symposia, etc., organized alternately for this purpose in different countries around the world.

7.1. The debate surrounding the Afro-Anglicanism movement

The Afro-Anglican movement is one of the fruits of the effort to "de-Anglicanize" Anglicanism. It is an effort to bring Anglicanism out of Anglo-Saxon captivity, particularly in African environments.

The first meeting was held in Barbados, South Africa in 1985 on the theme: *"Afro-*

anglicanism: Present Issues, Future Tasks". The aim was to reflect together on the place and role to be played by the African Anglican Church within the Anglican Communion on the one hand, and on the other, its place and role as a messenger of the Good News for the liberation of this continent from all dehumanizing structures. To this end, the participants were to discuss Africa's current challenges and outline prospects for the future.

This first meeting of African Anglicans was the beginning of a genuine African awareness of the role Africans must play in giving Anglicanism an African image.

This was followed by a second meeting in Cape Town, South Africa, in November 1996, on the theme of *"Afro-Anglicanism: Identity, Integrity and Impact in the Decade of Evangelism"*. On that occasion, George Carey, then Archbishop of Canterbury, said: "This Conference is a significant sign of that development (i.e.'the wonderful diversity we enjoy and also the underlying spirit of mutual love which binds us together'). The growing interest of the African tradition within the Communion is one of the most remarkable and exciting signs of the past thirty years. That you have gathered together from so many parts of the world at this time to celebrate our common roots, and I hope, to challenge one another and us all, with your discussions and your resolutions, is very encouraging"(l).

Our translation: "This conference is a sign of this development, that is, the wonderful diversity we rejoice in, and also underlines the spirit of mutual love that unites us together. The ever-growing interest in the African tradition within the Communion is one of the most remarkable and exciting signs of the past thirty years. The fact that you are coming together from different parts of the world at this time, to celebrate our common origins and, I hope, to challenge each other and all of us together in your discussions and resolutions, is very encouraging.

There is a growing need for Anglicanism to be assimilated by Africans. African Anglican leaders had gathered in South Africa to seek ways of forging a liturgy that employed indigenous expressions, rhythms, symbols and songs. For John Pobee, this would be the culmination of the inculturation of Anglicanism outside Anglo-Saxon culture. Ildit the following: "In my view, this is perhaps the most important aspect for inculturing Anglicanism in the non-Anglo context, because the majority of nonAnglos are not literate in the English language and idiom, and also because ritual is one of the cornerstones of religion" (2).

Our translation: "From my point of view, this is perhaps the most important aspect for the inculturation of Anglicanism in the non-English context, because the majority of non-English people are illiterate in the English language and idioms, and also because ritual is one of the cornerstones of religion".

Over the past thirty years, Anglican leaders on the dark continent have become increasingly aware of their responsibility to be heard within the Anglican Communion. While retaining traditional Anglican identity, the Afro-Anglican movement is joining other emancipatory movements in the quest for an identity for African Anglicanism.

Palpable signs of this are, among others, the translation of the Bible and the abundance of literature in local languages, the taking into account of the cultural aspects of each people, the desire to carry the Good News throughout the world (today, there are Blacks who are Bishops in certain Anglican Dioceses in the West) and the promotion of African theology.

The aim is to introduce the universal Church to the theological activities currently flourishing within the African Church. As can be seen, the concern of Afro-Anglicanism is not to wrestle with its roots, but rather to seek ways and means of establishing a new paradigm that can delight all members of the Anglican Communion.

7.2.   A place for the French-speaking world in the Anglican Communion

To signal their presence within the Anglican Communion and to defend the rights of French-speaking Anglicans, the Executive Council of the Churches of the Communion anglicane d'expression française was created in 1996.

It was a fight for recognition of the "Francophonie" within the Anglican Communion and the creation of the Association Internationale Rencontres, whose figurehead, the Reverend Canon

Jacques Bossière, greatly facilitated the struggle.

The "Rencontres" association was founded in 1985 by Canon Jacques Bossière, a French-born Episcopal priest. Noting the state of cultural abandonment of French-speaking Anglican churches, particularly in Africa (nearly 3 million Anglican Christians worldwide are French-speaking), Canon Bossière founded the association while fighting for recognition of the French language in the official bodies of the Anglican Communion.

" *Rencontres International* " is a private international association and a Non-Governmental Organization (NGO) in consultation with the United Nations. It has enabled the leaders of the French-speaking churches of the Anglican Communion to meet on several occasions, and to set up training, theological education, translation, equipment and mutual aid initiatives in many different forms. Consultations with French-speaking Anglicans continue on a regular basis, with the meeting place changing from country to country.

Delegates from the Anglican Church of Congo took an active part in all the meetings, and some of them even held positions of great responsibility in this Anglican Francophone organization. These include Mgr Henri Isingoma Kahwa and Mgr Zacharie Masimango Katanda, the current Vice-President of the Francophone Network, the President being Mgr Pierre Wallon, Bishop of the American Cathedral in Paris, France.

The first International Conference on French-speaking Anglicanism took place in Limuru, Kenya, from March 12 to 17, 1996 (see Proceedings of the Limuru Colloquium, Kenya), bringing together, for the first time, representatives from all the French-speaking countries where Anglicanism is active, and the organization of the Executive Council of the French-speaking world within the Anglican Communion.

The aim of this first meeting was to take stock of the French-speaking Anglican population worldwide (around three million and some forty bishops) and, above all, to ensure a living link between the dioceses and communities of all countries, a renewal of trust and a new dynamic of work and progress. The meeting also saw the creation of the "*Conseil Exécutif de la Francophonie Anglicane*".

The second international conference on French-speaking Anglicanism was held July 16-17, 1998 in Canterbury, England. This conference had brought together some forty bishops who had come for the Lambeth Conference in 1998, which began 2 days after this Colloquium organized by the Executive Council for the French-speaking world within the Anglican Communion (see Proceedings of the Colloquium in Canterbury, Great Britain.

Other conferences were held in Paris on the theme of reconciliation (in 2000), in Mauritius (in 2003) and in Montreal, Canada (in 2005).

But the fight for recognition of the presence of more than 3 to 4 million within the Anglican Communion, has so far only come to fruition at the Anglican Consultative Council Meeting *Anglican Consultative Council* Meeting (ACC-12) held in Hong Kong from 14 to 25 June. September 2002, which recognized the reality of the Anglican Francophonie in its Resolution n°17, by including the *Executive Council of the Francophonie*, as a "Francophone Network", among its working bodies. In fact, it was on the way to this Hong Kong meeting that Reverend Basimaki, priest of the Diocese of Boga/RDC, then a member of ACC-12, was murdered in September 2002 , in the village of Kyabwohe, in the vicinity of Bogasurlaroute. Uganda.

The member churches of this francophonie are:
- Indian Ocean Province (Mauritius, Seychelles, Reunion and Madagascar);
- Burundi Province;
- The Province of Rwanda ;
- Congo Province (Congo/Kinshasa and Congo/Brazzaville);
- The Church of Guinea/Conakry
- French-speaking parishes in the Western Province (Cameroon) ;
- The Church of Haiti and Haitian parishes in the USA;
- Les Doyennés francophones de l'Eglise anglicane du Canada ;

- French-speaking communities   in mainland France and in various   missions abroad.

around the world.

There are countries where the French language is used for communication, but where the Anglican Church is predominantly or predominantly English (e.g. Canada, Haiti, the Indian Ocean islands, and some West African countries such as Guinea/Conakry, Cameroon, etc.). In other countries, Anglican dioceses simply depend on other English-speaking provinces. This is the case in Haiti, which is dependent on the United States, or in Canada, which is English-speaking from the point of view of the Anglican Church.

It should be noted that, despite the French-speaking vocation of the Central African provinces, French is not the main language of worship, which is celebrated more in local languages, in line with the requirements of the Anglican Church. The same is true of former British colonies, where local languages are more widely used.

The minority position of these French-speaking provinces of Central Africa within the Anglican Communion has been very detrimental. All important Church documents, instructions, minutes of major meetings such as the Lambeth Conference or the Anglican Consultative Council, and even all books on Anglican theology, the history of Anglicanism, liturgy and other useful documentation, are all written in English. French speakers, who know nothing of English, are thus deprived of these intellectual and spiritual riches. All the good Anglican missionary training schools in the former British colonies and in the West also use English, and French speakers have no access to them. They are thus handicapped by the language factor.

During the 1998 Lambeth Conference, the French language was used informally in the Plenary Session. The tone was set by His Grace Michael Peers, Archbishop Primate of Canada, who in turn led the discussions in French. French speakers were able to ask their questions in French, and non-French speakers were encouraged to put their earphones to their ears. This was a great help to the bishops of Zaire, who don't have a good command of English, and to those of certain other French-speaking countries. The Francophones demanded and obtained French translations of all the minutes of meetings, books and other important documents of the Anglican Communion. And for the first time, simultaneous interpretation was provided in Swahili (for the wives), Spanish and Japanese.

8. The integration of Kinshasa's Nigerian Anglican community into the EAC

The first English service at Kinshasa's Saint Peter's Cathedral parish took place on June 13, 2010.

On May 20, 2010, Echezona Chukwuka Mbadugha (a Nigerian catechist) called a meeting of Nigerian Anglicans living in Kinshasa and explained his intention to start the Anglican Church in Kinshasa, as he felt that the community was not functional in the city. As Protestants, they decided to apply to the Protestant Centenary Cathedral for space in a school to start their Anglican Church.

On Sunday May 23, 2010, a 4-person delegation visited the Centenary Cathedral. After the service, they spoke with the pastor who had led the service, who asked them to return on Tuesday, May 25, 2010, the date of the pastors' meeting. The delegation was to return again on Saturday, May 29, 2010, as another pastors' meeting was scheduled for Friday.

On Saturday, the Nigerian delegation did indeed return, and the pastor in charge informed them that there was an Anglican church in Kinshasa, and gave them the address. The delegation immediately went to the address. There they met Evangelist Israël Kibonge, who advised them to meet Bishop Jean Botola Molanga on Sunday, May 30, 2010.

After this commemorative service dedicated to the life and work of Apolo Kivebulaya, the Nigerian delegation met with the Bishop, who was delighted with their presence.Bishop Jean Botola Molanga told them that the Anglican Church of Nigeria is a great Church, and that there must certainly be many Nigerian Anglicans among Kinshasa's foreign traders. "We were also looking for you, but unfortunately we didn't know who to ask," he added.

During the meeting on June 3, 2010, Evangelist Echezona announced to the Nigerian Anglicans the news of the discovery of the Anglican Church of Kinshasa, which was ready to welcome them into its midst, to everyone's great joy. Around 30 people took part in the meeting, during which they realized that, for good worship, the church needed a synthesizer and appropriate lighting. They then made a voluntary contribution, and the instruments were available for the following Sunday.

It was in this atmosphere that the Nigerian Anglican Community celebrated its first service in English, on June 13, 2010, at Saint Peter's Cathedral in Kinshasa. From an initial attendance of 30 on the first day, participation quickly grew to an average of 220 members each Sunday. The Community is an integral part of the Anglican Church of Congo.

It should also be noted that it was the visibility of the Anglican Church of Congo in Kinshasa, from 2004 onwards, that made this reunion possible.

Evangelist Echezona Chukwuka Mbadugha was ordained a deacon on December 8, 2013, by His Grace Katty at Saint Paul's Cathedral in Port Hacourt, Rivers State, Nigeria. On August 3, 2014, he was ordained a priest at Saint Pierre Cathedral in Kinshasa (DRC) by His Grace Henri Kahwa Isingoma. He will serve at the Cathedral Parish of Kinshasa in English-speaking worship and in the supervision of the Nigerian Anglican Community of Kinshasa.

But the community's activities are also evident in Kinshasa's other Lingalaphone parishes.

Here are some notable achievements of the Nigerian Anglican community in Kinshasa in the development of the Anglican Church of Congo in Kinshasa, under the dynamic leadership of Reverend Echezona:

- Completion of the provincial administration building and   the the Anglican church in the Commune of Kalamu;
- Planting a church at Bibwa in the N'sele Commune, Kinshasa;
- Planting a church in the city of Brazzaville, Republic of Congo;
- Purchase of a bus for the Church ;
- Substantial contribution to the purchase of a new plot of land, in the Commune of Ngiri-Ngiri, for the construction of a church and its outbuildings, for the Diocese of Kinshasa;
- Organization of an evangelization campaign in Matadi, Central Kongo Province.
- Punctual intervention in all church activities, at the request of hierarchical authorities or spontaneously.

The arrival of the Nigerian Anglican Community has been a great breath of fresh air for the Diocese of Kinshasa.

9. Contribution of bidders , foreign churches and partners to the development of the Anglican Church of Congo

The contribution of expatriate missionaries and partners to the revitalization and development of the evangelical works of the Anglican Church of Congo, in various fields, is very appreciable.

9.1. Missionary societies

9.1.1. The Church Missionary Society (CMS) of England

The work of the Church Missionary Society of England (CMS) within the Anglican Church of the Congo is remarkable. Indeed, the CMS of Great Britain has been the Anglican Church of Congo's primary partner since its establishment in Mboga in 1894 by Ugandan missionaries. It was indeed under the aegis and responsibility of the CMS that this Church arrived in the Democratic Republic of Congo, from Uganda, which was itself under the supervision of the Church of England.

We have said that the CMS is an old missionary Society founded in 1799 in London. It was the first to send missionaries to Uganda, at the request of Henry Morton Stanley in 1875. The first detachment of CMS missionaries arrived in Uganda on June 30, 1877. It was these CMS missionaries who had the right of oversight over the fledgling church in Mboga, Congo. In Apolo Kivebulaya's day, they often came to Mboga to administer the sacraments (Baptism and Confirmation) and other pastoral acts. After Apolo's death in 1933, they settled on the Mboga mission site from 1933 to 1960, managing the church with the help of the Diocese of Ruwenzori in Uganda, on which the Mboga ecclesiastical entity depended. Thus, from 1896 until Congo's independence in 1960, the Anglican Church of Congo was placed under the supervision of the CMS.

It was only after independence that the CMS handed over the baton of command and responsibility for running the Church to Congolese leaders in January 1967. Although many missionaries had returned to England after the Congo's accession to national and international sovereignty, the CMS had not abandoned the Anglican Church of the Congo, in which it still plays the role of *aima mater to* some extent.

If the Church often signs assistance contracts with certain missionary societies or organizations , for a fixed period of time , renewable or not, it's important to remember that it's not always possible for the Church to sign such contracts.
no such time-limited contract exists between the Anglican Church of Congo and CMS/England.

The partnership between the Anglican Church of Congo and CMS consists firstly in presenting to God the needs of evangelization on the mission field, praying for each other. Secondly, CMS continues to seek out and send missionaries with diverse skills, according to the need and demand of each Diocese of the Anglican Church of Congo. However, their numbers were considerably reduced after the years of Congolese independence, for two reasons: on the one hand, the EAC, having already trained many of its staff with acceptable skills, was able to manage or conduct certain Church affairs on its own. On the other hand, CMS is currently experiencing great difficulty in finding missionaries, as the vocation for mission is still quite strong, but the availability of people who speak French or are willing to learn the language has diminished.

The French language is a great challenge and sometimes a great obstacle for English speakers, as learning a language requires a considerable investment of time, effort and resources.

The CMS therefore prefers to intervene, insofar as it is able, in the strengthening of local skills, by providing them with support and the necessary material or financial aids, which can facilitate their ministry and other initiatives or projects for the development of the Church and the local Community: scholarships for studies at home or abroad, material and financial support for Bible schools, training or refresher seminars, meetings as well as the holding of certain important diocesan or provincial meetings, support for Church administration, travel facilities, etc.

It should be noted that the CMS/England works in several countries in Africa, Asia, South America, etc., and cannot alone carry such a burden for the Church in the DRC and Congo-Brazzaville. In addition to CMS/England's invaluable support and assistance, the Anglican Church in Congo also benefits from the support of other missionary societies, churches, organizations, etc.

9.1.2. The Church Missionary Society of Australia

The story of the development of the relationship between the Church Missionary Society/Australia and the Anglican Church of Zaire dates back to 1983, when the Reverend Peter Dawson, Missionary Personnel Secretary of the Church Missionary Society of Australia, met Bishop Dirokpa BalufUga of the Diocese of Bukavu in Zaire by chance in the CPK Guest House in Nairobi, Kenya. During the exchange, Bishop Dirokpa pleaded for missionaries to be sent to Zaire, where the needs were so great and the Church was in difficulty.

On his return to Australia, Reverend Dawson passed on this request for missionaries to the CMSA, who saw fit to obtain more information, for example: where the missionaries might be located, what they would be doing, how they would be housed, etc.

In October 1984, Reverend Dawson visited Zaire with Mr. Ross Hall (CMSA missionary in Tanzania). They stayed in Bukavu for a week, visiting churches, schools and dispensaries. They then travelled to Boga, where they spent four days.

As a result of the information gathered, it was decided to go ahead and look for recruits. Peter prepared an audio-visual presentation to be shown at CMS Summer Schools across Australia in January 1985. The presentation required a team of Bible teachers and other professionals such as doctors, builders, teachers, etc.

In mid-1985, a second visit was made by Ross Hall and the Reverend Dr. Canon Alan Cole, Federal Secretary of the WCSA. They visited Bukavu, then traveled by road to Boga via Goma and Butembo.

Peter Dawson made a third preparatory visit in September 1986, travelling first to Boga and then, with Pat Nickson, by road to Bukavu via Butembo, Rutshuru and Goma.

The first WCSA missionaries to arrive in Zaire were David and Prudence Boyd, with their two-year-old daughter Emily, in Bukavu on December 10, 1986.

We can therefore say that the Anglican Church of Congo's partnership with the *Church Missionary Society/Australia* dates back to 1983, but the missionary activities themselves began in 1986.

Table 3 in the Appendix lists the names of all Australian missionaries who worked in the Anglican Church of the Congo, their occupation and place of work, and the year of arrival and return of each of them to Australia.

A large number of CMSA missionaries came to the Diocese of Bukavu between 1986 and 1996, and *ipso facto*, the Dioceses of Nord-Kivu and Kindu benefited from them, as they were, at the time, Archdeaconries of the Diocese of Bukavu.

Here is the testimony of Mr. Ross Hall, sent on March 20, 2016, to Reverend David Boys, CMSA missionary in Bukavu:

"I found, during fifteen years as CMSA Missionary Personnel Secretary, during which I visited over 20 countries and met many bishops, other leaders, heads of institutions, etc., that Bishop Dirokpa was the most hospitable and best organized of all. Bishop Dirokpa was the most hospitable and best organised of them all. I would like Bishop Dirokpa to know this". Regards, Ross.

[I found, in the fifteen years I spent as Secretary of the Missionary Staff of the CMSA, during which time I visited over 20 countries and met many bishops, other religious leaders, heads of institutions, etc., that Bishop Dirokpa was the most welcoming and organized of them all. Bishop Dirokpa was the most welcoming and well-organized of all. I would like Bishop Dirokpa to know this].

9.1.3. The Church Missionary Society of Ireland (CMSI)

The Missionary Society sent a missionary couple to the Diocese of Bukavu in 1991. They were the Reverends Georges and Anne Pitt, accompanied by their little boy, Luc. They built two Bible schools in semi-durable materials, one in Kiwanza/Rutshuru (North Kivu) and the other in Bangwe/Uvira (South Kivu), each with classrooms, a dormitory for students and accommodation for the Director. The Reverend Georges Pitt was himself the Director of the Kiwanza Bible School and taught, with his wife Anne, in the same establishment. At the same time, he also supervised Bible teaching at the Bangwe Bible School and reported to the Bishop of the Diocese of Bukavu. During their three-year contract, George and Anne Pitt performed brilliantly in the Diocese of Bukavu. CMSI has also often intervened on an ad hoc basis, at the request of the diocesan bishop. However, the level of intervention is not comparable to that of the CMS/England or the CMSA.

9.1.4. Mid-Africa Ministry (MAM) or Rwanda Mission

The Mid-Africa Ministry is a missionary Society initiated in England, with the aim of assisting the Anglican Church of Rwanda and Burundi in their evangelization needs. For this reason, it was called *"Rwanda Mission"* when it was founded. But when the Province of Burundi, Rwanda and Zaire (PRBZ) was created in 1980, the bishops of Rwanda, in particular, and those of Burundi, rebelled against this appellation, which emphasized the name of their country, as if the *Rwanda Mission* alone satisfied all their ministry needs. They felt that this name was detrimental to their mission because, in their view, because it characterized or categorized assistance or aid solely to the Church of Rwanda, the other partners no longer supported them as they should, given that for all projects coming from the Churches of these two countries, they always referred them to the *Rwanda Mission*.

The *Rwanda Mission* was thus forced to abandon this name. This missionary society was christened *Mid-Africa Ministry* (MAM). From then on, the Society was to work not only in Rwanda and Burundi, but also in south-western Uganda and the DRC, where it had sent two missionaries to Boga: Miss Pat Clay and Dr Charlotte Plieth. From then on, his impact on the mission fields was minimal, at least in the Anglican Church of Congo.

9.1.5. Congo Church Association (CCA)

The *Congo Church Association* (CCA) is not a missionary society like its predecessors, but an organization or association of men of good will set up to support the Anglican Church of Congo in its evangelizing mission.

Indeed, the *Congo Church Association* was founded by Bishop Philip Ridsdale, the first Bishop of the Diocese of Boga, immediately after his retirement in the 1980s. He had remained preoccupied by the alarming situation of poverty in the Anglican Church, with its enormous needs, not only material or financial, but also in human resources, i.e. the preparation of personnel with a good intellectual, moral and spiritual formation, with a view to supporting the Church in its rapid expansion towards the major centers and cities of the country, for a holistic evangelization.

Bishop Philip Ridsdale knew that the Church of Uganda also had its own organization, called *the Uganda Church Association* in Great Britain, so he wanted to provide the EAC with a similar organization in the DRC, with specific aims: to advance the Christian religion and alleviate poverty among the clergy and their families. The CCA was to provide information about the Church in the DRC and encourage others to pray for the Anglican Church in Congo. It was also concerned to provide funds for even a modest pension for EAC clergy at the end of their ministerial careers. The CCA also set itself the goal of seeking funds for the specific needs of the EAC, and in particular for the Institut Supérieur Théologique Anglican (ISThA), now the Université Anglicane du Congo (UAC), and so on.

The CCA itself is fed by various sources of support from individuals and some organizations. The CCA gave each Diocese the opportunity to visit its Jersey partner in 1998 and 2008, to establish a better program of collaboration and assistance. Also worth mentioning here are the Old Catholics in Holland and Switzerland, the Episcopal Church in the USA and various individuals in Britain and the USA who have some links with the DRC. On more than one occasion, Mgr Philip has visited the United States, sometimes accompanied by the Reverend Canon Bill Norman, to raise funds.

EncreantlaCCA   ,   MgrPhilipRisdalealsowantedtopaulCMS/England
in its onerous task of providing assistance, the main focus of which will henceforth be on sending missionaries, supporting them on the mission field and providing some training grants. The CCA wanted to help the growing dioceses of the EAC and respond to their particular needs.

Alongside the CCA, the Reverend Canon William (Bill) Norman, as General Commissioner of the Anglican Church of the Congo in England, who worked closely with the CCA committee, is to be congratulated on his enormous efforts. Together, we were able to manage the funds raised very well and distribute them judiciously among the Dioceses of the DRC, according to the needs presented. The Reverend Canon Bill Norman played this delicate role with the heart of a good father from 1993 until his retirement in 2011.

We should also mention the enormous assistance given to the Anglican Church of Congo by Bishop Michael Scott-Joynt, Bishop of Winchester and patron of CCA: his friendship and spiritual and pastoral support for EAC leaders, as well as his considerable advocacy in the House of Lords (British Parliament), where he often drew the government's attention to atrocities and injustices during the war years in the DRC.

Here are the main personalities who have led and managed this organization from its inception to the present day:

- **Chairman of the CCA Committee** :
  - Mgr Philip Ridsdale 1980-1997
  - Reverend Canon Jeremy Pemberton 1997-2007
  - Ms Judy Rous 2007 to date...
- **CCA Sponsor** :
  - Mgr Leslie Brown 1987-2000
  - Bishop Philip Ridsdale 1997-2000
  - Michael Scott-Joynt, Bishop of Winchester, 2000-2014
  - Deaconess Lucy Ridsdale 2002-2011
  - Bishop David Williams, Bishop of Basingstoke in the Diocese of Winchester, 2016.

9.1.6. Overseas churches, African churches and organizations

In addition to the support provided by missionary societies and the *Congo Church*

Association, the Anglican Church of the Congo also benefits from the contribution and support of other churches in the West, America and Africa, in the establishment and consolidation of evangelical works and the development of the Church and its people in various fields: material and financial support, scholarships, construction, sending missionaries, facilitating major meetings or gatherings of the Church through financial intervention in travel and organization expenses, financing projects initiated by the Church for itself or in favor of the population, discretionary funds, natural disasters and emergencies, etc.

These include the Episcopal Church in the USA and Canada, the Office of the Archbishop of Canterbury, the Anglican Churches of Uganda, Kenya, Tanzania and Nigeria, which had sent missionaries to the DRC, and others, as well as a number of Church organizations: Trinity Church Grant (Ecusa), Episcopal Relief and Development (ERD), Anglican Relief and Development Fund (ARDF)/USA, Etre Partenaires, TearFund, Christian Aid, etc.

Considering the list of partners and their areas of intervention, many would think that the EAC is spoiled for choice in its mission of evangelization and development. This is true, but in the field, the scope of action is vast and efforts seem to be scattered. As a result, the impact of aid and support can only be seen here and there. The Church has not yet left the poverty zone. It is still in need, but there is a clear improvement and progress, albeit slow but decisive. With sincere thanks, the EAC wishes to continue this partnership in mission.

9.1.7. Christian businessmen

The Anglican Church of Congo has also benefited from the contribution and support of a number of well-intentioned Christian businessmen, who have not hesitated to make part of their assets available to the Church. Here are just a few examples.

A special place must be reserved for the family of Mr. *Philp Betts* and his wife *Deborah*, a Christian businessman of British origin currently based in Kampala, Uganda, whose contribution is remarkable in the Dioceses of Bukavu, Nord-Kivu and Kindu. They previously lived in Goma.

Saint Paul's parish church in Goma was built during the time of Reverend Munzenda and Mr. Josias Nkusi, who supervised the work. The Betts family made a significant contribution to the work.

The construction of the Ndahura Institute in Goma. This was made possible thanks to the contribution of Edm Schluter & Co, Esco Kivu's parent company, which provided the land. In 1993, Reverend Masimango built the school with the support of a committee made up of Philip Betts, Malcolm Richards and Josias Nkusi. The first phase of work cost $25,750, and $24,560 was budgeted for the second phase. Contributors included Maranatha Trust (UK), Philip and Deborah Betts, Zaire Church Association, Malcolm Richard, Jeremy and Jill Lawson, several other Englishmen and local contributions. A further donation of $8,700 was received from Maranatha Trust for the rehabilitation of the Ndahura Institute in June 2009.

It should also be noted that during the eruption of the Nyiragongo volcano in 2002, the Betts family received several donations from England, including food, clothing, tarpaulins, blankets, etc., which they handed over to Reverend Assumani Kirunga for distribution.

Erection of the Archdeacon's house in Goma: This house was built by Reverend Assumani from May 30, 2002 to June 2003. It cost about $16,500. The main contributors were: Philip and Deborah Betts, Congo Church Association, CMS, Reverend Jérémie (UK), Reverend John (Chicago), Reverend Malcolm, Mgr Masimango, Reverend Mbusa and local contributions. It included 6 bedrooms, 2 WCs, a large living room, a dining room and two balconies. This house will soon serve as the office of the Diocese of Goma's Bishopric, the inauguration of which will take place on November 20, 2016 with the consecration of its Iᵉ Bishop, Mgr Désiré Mukanirwa Kadorho.

The Betts family donated musical instruments to Saint Paul's parish church in Goma, Radio Sauti ya Injili in Goma, Saint Peter's Cathedral in Bukavu, Saint André's Cathedral in Butembo, Saint Peter's Cathedral in Kinshasa and Kindu Cathedral.

Many Anglican students have also benefited from Philip Betts scholarships for training at the CCLK (Centre Chrétien du Lac Kivu training Evangelists for one year). They come from all the EAC dioceses. A theology student from the Diocese of Butembo received a scholarship to study at the Anglican University of Congo (UAC) in Bunia.

Around a hundred Anglican servants have undergone their training in Mission, Evangelism, Discipleship and Development at the Center. Some are priests or Diocesan and Parish Coordinators in the Office of Evangelism, making a big impact in church planting in both rural and urban areas, and in proclaiming the Good News of Jesus Christ.

To this day, the Betts family provides regular financial support to radio sauti ya injili in Goma, the CCLK in Goma, the Diocese of Kindu, the widows of the Anglican Church of Congo in Goma, and the project for girls and women run by Reverend Désiré Mukanirwa Kadhoro in Goma.

The contribution of other Congolese Christian businessmen is also noteworthy:

In Beni, Madame Bonabana, the wife of a Greek subject, built the parish church of Saint Jean de Kasabinyole under the supervision of Reverend Balinda in 1980.

In Butembo, Mr. Chuma, later appointed Canon of Saint André Cathedral in Butembo, built the building with the help of other local businessmen, under the supervision of Canon Kabonabe, then Archdeacon of Butembo, in .....

In Kamango, Mr. Baliesima Albert, currently a national deputy, and his wife Maman Marthe Vjra, along with other men of good will, built the Diocese of Kamango bishopric in 2015.

10. The visits of the Archbishops of Canterbury to the Province of the Anglican Church of Congo

10.1. His Grace Robert Runcie's stay in Bukavu

His Grace Robert Runcie, Archbishop of Canterbury, arrived in the Diocese of Bukavu on May 11, 1980 to inaugurate Africa's first French-speaking province, the *Province of the Anglican Church of Burundi, Rwanda and '/.a'ire (PBRZ)*.

During his stay in Bukavu, the Archbishop of Canterbury presided over the enthronement ceremonies of the 1er Archbishop of this new Province, in the person of Mgr Ndahura Bezaleri, Bishop of Bukavu. He was assisted by His Grace Silvanus Wani, Archbishop of the Church of Uganda, who had thus granted autonomy to the new French-speaking province, which had remained under the jurisdiction of the Church of Uganda for 84 years.

10.2. His Grace Rowan Williams visits Bunia and Boga

His Grace Rowan Williams, Archbishop of Canterbury, arrived in Bunia on Friday June 24, 2011, for a 4-day pastoral visit to the Anglican Church of the Democratic Republic of Congo. While appreciating the work of Apolo Kivebulaya, pioneer of the Anglican Church of Congo, he asked about the inspirational work of the Church, helping individuals and the community to rebuild their lives after the trauma of years of conflict.

During his stay, Dr Williams was able to meet a group of young people who had been abducted from school to join the militia, but who had been returned to their families thanks to an Anglican Church organization called "AGAPE", which transformed their lives through faith and compassion. It was clear from their personal testimonies that their priority, in reality, was to complete their studies. Many of them were asking to return to secondary school, even though they were now older than their classmates.

On June 25, 2011, the Archbishop of Canterbury made a round trip from Bunia to Boga. His Grace the Archbishop was greeted by the local chief and the local population. After worship and celebration at Saint Apolo Cathedral   , he   met   with several hundred
of natives, including Pygmies, who had come to tell of their expulsion from the forest they considered their home. They had already lived in limbo for two years, with no sign of their displacement coming to an end.

In the cathedral garden, Dr. Williams had spoken to a group of women who had suffered severely from the atrocities perpetrated by militias, which had led to stigmatization and isolation by their families and the whole community. The Anglican Church had responded to the endemic sexual violence against women by creating a women's association. Working in collaboration with the Mothers' Union
(*Mothers' Union*), this association campaigns against violence and stigmatization. It also provides practical assistance, helping women to reach the nearest health center within 72 hours of the attack,

for HIV preventive treatment.

Sunday June 26, 2011 was reserved for Sunday worship in Bunia.

Commenting on the visit, His Grace Henri Isingoma, Archbishop of the Province of the Anglican Church of Congo, said: "Your visit has strengthened the fraternal relations of communion between the Anglican Province of Congo and the other provinces of the Anglican Communion. At home, we say 'the true friend is the one we see in times of distress'. For the Congolese people, you are a brother, because of your pastoral care for us, like a spiritual father".

At the end of his visit, Dr Williams said: "What I had the opportunity to see of the work of the Anglican Church in Congo was very moving and inspiring. This is a Church that is really making a difference to very wounded and vulnerable people, in an emerging society that is still precarious, emerging from a period of terrible collective trauma. They need encouragement and support - but we need their vision and compassion even more.

The Archbishop of Canterbury left Bunia on Monday June 27, 2011 for London.

10.3. His Grace Justin Welby's visit to Goma

His Grace Justin Welby visited DR Congo in February 2014, as part of the Great Lakes Peace Program. This is an ecumenical initiative of the Anglican Church and the Roman Catholic Church of Burundi, the Democratic Republic of Congo and Rwanda, supported by Caford and Peace One Day, among others.

During his missionary tour of the Great Lakes countries, His Grace Justin Welby, Archbishop of Canterbury, arrived in the Democratic Republic of Congo, accompanied by his wife Caroline Welby, on February 03, 2014. He had just completed similar visits to South Sudan, Rwanda and Burundi, via Uganda.

In Goma, he was welcomed at the big barrier on the border with Rwanda by His Grace Henri Isingoma Kahwa, Archbishop of the Province of the Anglican Church of Congo/Kinshasa and Congo/Brazzaville, and Mgr Bahati Bali-Busane, Bishop of the Diocese of Bukavu, as well as the Vicar General of the Catholic Diocese of Goma, surrounded by the clergy and faithful of local religious denominations.

After a short rest at the Hotel Ihusi in Goma, he went to the Anglican parish of St. Paul in Goma for a service of thanksgiving. The service was attended by a large number of Christians and leaders from the Catholic Church and several   Protestant denominations in Goma .
reconciliation". His message was well received by the congregation, as it was appropriate for a time when the inhabitants of Goma (Gomatracians) needed consolation and biblical exhortation, especially as they had just spent some very difficult years under the bombs, killings and acute trauma caused by the war of the March 23 Movement (M23).

During his three-day stay in the tourist town of Goma, Archbishop Justin Welby met with various sections of the population to discuss the   warlike situation prevailing   in North   Kivu   at   the time   .
The Archbishop's program was as follows:

- On February 3, 2014, he met with Archbishop Isingoma to exchange views on the situation of the Anglican Church in DR. Congo and on the ecclesiological crisis within the worldwide Anglican communion;
- February   4, 2014   , from 8:00   to   10:00   a.m.: Ilareçulesleadersdesconfessions

  The Archbishop of Canterbury was invited to meet with a number of religious leaders who explained the problems arising from the recurring wars in the east of the Democratic Republic of Congo. They requested the support of the Archbishop of Canterbury in their efforts to seek peace;
- On February 4, 2014, at precisely 10 a.m. on that same Wednesday, the Archbishop was received, for pleasantries, in the office of the Governor of the Province of North Kivu, by Mr. Julien Paluku Kahongya.

  At 11 a.m., the Archbishop visited displaced persons in the Mugunga camp, where he felt first-hand their misery. Having prayed for them, he pledged his support by getting involved in the search for peace in the country.

On the evening of the same day, the Archbishop took part in a reception organized in his honor by the Archbishop of the Province of the Anglican Church of Congo (PEAC) at the Hotel Ihusi in Goma. Numerous political, administrative and religious authorities, including the Governor of North Kivu, were also invited.

On February 5, 2014, Archbishop Justin Welby was joined by the British Ambassador to DR. Congo. Together, they visited the sick and women victims of sexual violence at the Heal Africa hospital before leaving Goma in the afternoons.

Archbishop Justin Welby's visit was so important that it erased any confusion from the minds of people unfamiliar with the Anglican Church. Similarly, his preaching on a difficult theme, after war and hatred, brought some souls back to repentance for peaceful cohabitation. Anglican Christians in the DRC were delighted to commune with the spiritual Father of the Anglican Communion.

11. Resolutions of the eighth Provincial Synod of the Anglican Church of Congo in February 2016 in Bunia/Muhito

For information purposes, we have selected a number of resolutions from the Eighth Provincial Synod that we consider important. We have included their numbers as they appear in the Acts of the Synod.

3. The Synod decides that the Archbishop-elect remains Bishop of his Diocese as specified in the EAC Constitution (revised). The national headquarters of the EAC remains established in Kinshasa as stipulated in the EAC Constitution, section 2, article 2.

6. The Synod adopts the revised EAC constitution and undertakes to abide by it.

8. The Synod mandates the Archbishop to appoint, with the approval of the College of Bishops, a National Chancellor of the EAC, for the management of judicial files and legal representation.

12. The Synod approves the Archbishop's resignation and resolves that the College of Bishops be convened, in three months' time, to elect a new Archbishop of the EAC.

13. The Anglican Church of Congo maintains its doctrinal teaching based on the Bible, against all non-orthodox theological currents.

14. With regard to the creation of new Dioceses and missionary Dioceses, the Synod decides:
   a. **Goma**: accepts that the Diocese of Bukavu will soon organize the elective synod for the Diocese of Goma.
   b. **Brazzaville**: agreed that Brazzaville should be erected as a missionary diocese to spread the Gospel.
   c. **Kananga**: decides to wait for the report from the Diocese of Mbuji-Mayi for the two Kasais, which will be presented to the next EAC college to rule on the matter.
   d. **Kalemie**: decides to wait for the report from the Diocese of Katanga, at the end of its next diocesan synod, before ruling on the matter.
   e. **Kinshasa**: as Kinshasa is already a diocese according to the constitution, the synod is calling for a diocesan elective synod to be held in the very near future, to elect a diocesan bishop.
   f. **Béni**: accepts the request for the creation of the Diocese of Béni and asks the Diocese of North Kivu to organize the election of the Bishop at its 2018 Ordinary Synod.

19. The synod decides to remove the map of the DRC and the EAC emblem, since the mission goes beyond borders.

21. The Synod appoints Venerable Etsa Lombomba Richard, National Coordinator of Protestant Covenant Schools/11ᵉ CAC.

These resolutions are 90 percent complete as we hand over the manuscript of this work to the presses.

GENERAL CONCLUSION

The Anglican Church of the Congo, which began as a mustard seed in Congolese soil, had no inkling that it would one day grow into a giant tree (Mat.13:31). Implanted by Ugandan catechists, of whom Apolo Kivebulaya (1896-1933) remains the figurehead, it has held firm against all odds with the means at hand, with particular emphasis on evangelization. This proves that this is indeed the Church of God, where the Holy Spirit is at work and living faith is on the march.

During the post-Apolo Kivebulaya period (1933-1960), the Church came under the leadership of white missionaries from CMS/England, who took over the expanding work in Mboga. At this time, particular emphasis was placed on training God's servants and other catechists to consolidate the work begun by Apolo Kivebulaya.

This period was marked by three important events: the arrival of white missionaries in Mboga, promotion in the pastoral ministry and freedom of worship for all following Congo's independence.

When the Congo gained national and international sovereignty, the Anglican Church of the Congo came under the responsibility of Congolese leaders, while remaining under the ecclesiastical jurisdiction of Uganda. It obtained its civil personality from the Congolese government, under the name of : *Eglise anglicane congolaise* and its legal representatives were appointed by the same Presidential Order of December 1er 1960.

The Anglican Church, which had long operated in Mboga (1894-1960), gradually left its homeland after Congo's independence and reached the country's other major towns and cities. It expanded rapidly over large areas, in record time.

As part of its expansion, other autonomous Anglican churches were discovered, which reached the Congo by routes other than Boga's: Katanga, North Kivu, Kinshasa, Mahagi and Aru, Congo-Brazzaville. This was an opportunity to integrate everyone into the Anglican Church that had arrived via Mboga.

The Church was then faced with a shortage of trained personnel to look after new members, especially those from other churches and sects professing diversified doctrines; with insufficient financial means, etc. The EAC did not disarm in the face of these real difficulties. The EAC did not give up in the face of these very real difficulties. It has continually sought to overcome them with God's grace.

As far as worship was concerned, all liturgical documents were written in the Lunyoro language. As the Church expanded, these documents were translated first into Swahili, then Lingala and finally Tshiluba.

The EAC, conscious of its vocation to the holistic evangelization of the Church, had organized various development departments at diocesan and provincial levels.

The Church of Uganda, which itself became an autonomous ecclesiastical province in 1961, ceded more and more responsibility to the Congolese Church, notably through the creation of the Archdeaconry, the Diocese and the Francophone Council. The three French-speaking countries regained their autonomy from the Church of Uganda, forming the autonomous French-speaking Ecclesiastical Province of Burundi, Rwanda and Zaire (PBRZ). The Anglican Church of Zaire finally became an autonomous ecclesiastical province: La Province de L'Eglise Anglicane du Zaïre (PEAZ), which led the church to its centenary (1896-1996).

The so-called war of liberation waged by AFDL forces (1996-1997), followed by another so-called RCD war (1998), did not fail to destabilize the Church: refugees, loss of life, wicked destruction of Church infrastructures, etc. were all recorded. Another inter-tribal war, just as atrocious as the first, broke out in Ituri between Lendu and Hema (2001-2003) and caused the same damage.

Faced with the enormous difficulties of communication with home and abroad as a result of the war, the EAC opened a liaison office in Kampala in 1997 to coordinate the activities of the Anglican dioceses of the DRC.

Evangelization had not stopped. It continued its course despite many vicissitudes. Other Dioceses were created: Kindu (1997), Kinshasa (2003), Aru (2005), Kasai (2010), Kamango (2016), Goma (2016), Congo/Brazzaville (2016).

In its constant development, the evangelical works of PEAC/RDC crossed the border into the Republic of Congo/Brazzaville in 1997.

Interested by Apolo's recommendation on his sickbed in 1933, to see the evangelization he began in Mboga, cross the equatorial forest and reach the other end of the Congo, the EAC made this dream its own and brought the grain of the Good News all the way to the mouth of the Congo River, at Moanda /Banana (2005), in western DR Congo.

With a view to providing the Church with a framework for quality training, the EAC first created the Anglican Higher Theological Institute, which was later transformed into the "Université Anglicane du Congo" (UAC), with several faculties up to degree level. The aim was to meet the needs not only of the Church, but also of the local community. The first Congolese Anglican Doctors of Theology from the PEAC are also being trained, and are now taking over from our institutions of higher and university education.

Having now reached maturity, the EAC was visited by the Archbishops of Canterbury, Rowan Williams, who came to appreciate, on the ground, the work of Apolo Kivebulaya in Bogaand to console the population battered by wars and nameless violence. He was followed, 3 years later, by another Archbishop of Canterbury, Justin Welby, in Goma, for the opening of the Year of Peace in the Great Lakes Countries, with his peers from the Catholic Churches of the DRC, Burundi and Rwanda.

Despite some shortcomings inherent in any human endeavor, the record of the Anglican Church of Congo over the past 120 years in the field of evangelism in the Democratic Republic of Congo and Congo/Brazzaville is largely positive. The EAC is present in all 11 former provinces of the DRC. Although the number of Christians varies from region to region, the greatest concentration of Anglicans is to be found in the east of the country, where the Church has been evolving for a long time. All this is proof that those who have taken the baton from Apolo Kivebulaya's hands have honoured him by their assiduous work, in the long journey of evangelizing the DR Congo, for the glory of God.

Table 1: Missionaries who worked in the Diocese of Katanga, their functions and origins

N°	Name	Civil status	Wife's name	Nationality	Function	Arrival date	Departure date
1.	Tailor Zabriskie	M		American	Pasteur	1982	1984
2.	Ben	M		American	Pasteur	1985	1989
3.	Timothy Naish	M		British	Pasteur	1991	1992
4.	Claire	c		British	Sec. Special	1993	1996
5.	Dr Ross	M		British	Health coordinator	1994	1997
6.	Ms Sonia	c		Jewish	Health coordinator	1994	1997
7.	Judith Acheson	c		British	Nat. Coord. JCA	2003	2011
8.	Rebecca	c		British	BDC trainee	2004	2004
9.	Johanna	c		British	Trainee U.M	2008	2009
10.	Eric	M	Sandra	British	Health coordinator	2005	2010
11.	Mike	M	Nancy	British	Doctor	-	-
12.	Ian Harvey	c		British	Coord. Street children/ Kimbilio center	2009	2013
13.	Mull ensIan Andrew	c		British	Trainee at the Kimbilio center	2015	2016

Missionary New Zealand: Dr Carierons and Hilary (wife) = Doctor

Table 2. Brief history and evolution of the development and social works department of the anglican church of congo (eac): 1980-2016

Year	Archbishop	Key characters or main hosts	Comments and major achievements
1980 1981	SaGrâce Ndahura Bezaleri	Folkets (Development)	American missionary based in Bukavu. **Some achievements**: the Vitshumbi fishery in North Kivu and the Fizi sawmill in South Kivu.
1982 2002	His Grace Njojo Byankya	MissNyaka to Kabarole (Community Development Office). Ms Nyangoma Kabarole (Medical Department)	Based in Boga and renowned for its hospitality and transparent management. It benefited from the advisory and technical support of two British missionaries: Tim Rous and Bill Crooks. **Some achievements**: projects agropastoral, sawmill, transport of people and goods. Based in Boga and renowned for its dedication and credibility. She benefited from the advisory and technical support of Miss Pat Nickson, a British missionary who played a major role in the creation of the company , the organization, training and financing of the Medical Service. The Medical Service is also marked by the work of missionaries Dr Nigel P. , Mrs Christine D. (Surgeon), Mr Toulmin Graham
2003 2009	SaGrâce Dirokpa Balufuga Fidele	Mr Mushamuka HamisiF idele (BDC)	Based in Bukavu and supported by Tammi Mott, Bill Crooks, Jacques Birugurugu, Robert Kilonzo and Rev. Martin Nguba. Recognized for...............................
2010 2016	SaGrâce Isingoma Kahwa Henri		**Major achievements** : - **2003** in Kampala: strategic planning of the PEAC for the development of evangelism and

				and development.
				- **2003-2004**: emergency aid for Congolese refugees in Uganda fleeing massacres in Ituri
				- 2007-2016: Popularization of the ENP (Ensemble Nous Pouvons) approach, focusing on mobilizing the Church and the community for integral transformation with more local resources. Carried out with the financial and technical support of Episcopal Relief and Development and Tearfund.
				- **2010-2016** : With financial support from ARDF (AnglicanRelief and Development Fund): construction of two peace centers in Butembo and Bukavu, two schools in Boga and Bukavu, a professional carpentry center in Aru, and an orphanage in Butembo. Two agricultural projects in Kasai and Katanga
				- **2012-2014** in South Kivu: environmental protection through community reforestation. Financial support from Tearfund
				- **2014-2015**: food and non-food aid for hundreds of displaced people fleeing the Beni massacres; thousands of Burundian refugees in the DRC fleeing the violence; hundreds of flood victims in Kisangani; and hundreds of people affected by Cholera in Lubumbashi. In particular, with financial support from ERD (Episcopal Relief and Development), Tearfund, Anglican Aid, Congo Church Association (CCA);
				- **2013-2016**: Great Lakes Peace Program (ecumenical initiative of the Anglican and Catholic Churches of Burundi, DRC and Rwanda).

| | | MrBaliesima Kadukima Albert (Medical Service): 2003-2011 | Supported by CAFOD and Peace one day. |
| | | | -**2013-2016**: telecommunications project (installation of Internet cyber cafés in 9 Dioceses and at the Anglican University of Congo) with financial support from Trinity Church Wall Street in New York, **2014-2015** : Boga, North Kivu, Aru and South Kivu: project to prevent and combat sexual and gender-based violence. Supported by TearfUnd and Episcopal Relief and Development. **2016**: participation in the national synod, in the development of two important manuals: administrative and financial management manual (MAP AF) and resource mobilization manual. Recognized for his ability to mobilize resources and diversify health activities (in addition to fighting and preventing HIV/AIDS, supplying some communities with drinking water, etc.). He was supported by Dr Muliro, Mr Jean Claude Ngango Dirokpa and Dr Raymond Bombo, who succeeded him. |

Table 3: Church Missionary Society/Australia missionaries sent to the Anglican Church of Zaire/Democratic Republic of Congo

NAMES	PERIOD	LOCATION	DEPARTMENT
David and Prudence Boyd	December 1986 July 1996	Bukavu	David: Theological education by extension, Director of theological education, Bible teaching Prudence: Ministry to the deaf at the Center for the Handicapped, health and nutrition education, women's ministry
	June 2014 present	Bukavu	David: Bible teaching, preaching Prudence: Ministry to the deaf at the Center for the Handicapped and General Hospital
Brett and Raya Newell	Brett: March 1987 - August 1994 Raya:February 1988-August 1994	Butembo	Brett: Medical Director Raya: Ministry to teenage girls, teaching Bible and sewing, liaison with Mission Aviation Fellowship
Margaret Lawry	June 1987-November 1994	Bukavu	Training and seminars for pastors and lay church leaders, CMSA coordinator
David Alsop	June 1987 July 1990	Boga	Teacher at the Ecole Biblique, Chaplain at the Institut des Techniques Médicales
Geoffet Narelle Stanbury	July 1987 July 1996	Bukavu	Geoff: Bible teaching by cassette Narelle: Teaching, ministry for women
Graham and Wendy Toulmin	December 1987 February 1992	Butembo	Graham: Dental service in the medical department Wendy: Administration, literacy
	August 2015 - present	Aru	Graham: Head of the Dental Section at the Institut Supérieur des Techniques Médicales (ISTM) Wendy: Head of Dental Section Administration and iSTM Research Project Manager
Graham Toulmin made 12 private visits to Zaire / DRC between 1993 and 2014 to support the Dental Service.			
Brain and Ruth Fagan	October 1987 July 1996	Butembo	Brian: Building houses for missionaries, Bible teaching, preaching Ruth: Women's ministry, literacy, Bible teaching
Malcolm and Elizabeth Richards	July 1988 July 1989	Bukavu	Both: Help develop courses for Bible Schools, teaching, youth ministry

	July 1989 June 1994	Goma	Both: Youth ministry, evangelism, pastors' conferences Malcolm: Assistant Archdeacon (administration) Elizabeth: Women's ministry (sewing, ETE)
	September 2005 - December 2010	Kmdu	Both: Establish Beroya Bible School, Bible teaching, pastors' conferences, seminars Malcolm: Director of theological education Elizabeth: Teaching trauma healing
Ti cket Christine Screw	February 1991 - July 1996	Bukavu	Both: Training and seminars for pastors and lay church leaders
Pe teret Marie Dawson	February December 1992	Bukavu	Bible teaching, confirmation
	December 1992 - November 1996	Kmdu	Preparing the Maniema region to become a new Diocese
Maggie Crewes	November 1992 - December 1998	Butembo	Community nurse/midwife 1992-1994 Director of Medical Services 1994-1998
	August 1999 December 2002	-K ampala (Uganda)	Congo Liaison Office
Sue Jaggar	May 2007 June 2009	Kindu	Sunday School teacher training, teaching at Beroya Bible School

Short-term :

D ouglasand Dado Burroughs	June - December 1990	! Bukavu	Building a house for missionaries
M alcolmet Shelley Galbraith	January - October 1991	Butembo	Malcolm: Construction, youth ministry Shelley: Teaching Toulmin children, literacy
Kathryn Seebohm	August 1995 - July 1996	Butembo	Replacing Maggie Crewes as Medical Director

Dirokpa Balufuga Fideele is Archbishop Emeritus of the Ecclesiastical Province of the Anglican Church of Congo. He is the former Bishop of the Diocese of Bukavu (1982 - 2006) and the 1st Bishop of the Diocese of Kinshasa (2003 - 2009).

Before his ordination to the priesthood in 1980, he served in various departments of the Congolese government civil service, holding several positions up to the rank of director. He was a National Deputy in the 2e Legislature of the 2e Republic (1975). He also took part in the Mouvement Populaire de la Révolution (MPR) Congress in Nsele in 1990, initiating the multiparty system in Zaire; and was a member of the Conférence Nationale Souveraine (CNS) held in Kinshasa from 1991 to 1992.

After graduating with a B.A in Theology and Pastoral Studies from Oak Hill Theological College, Middlesex University, London in 1995, Mgr Dirokpa obtained his Doctorate in Theology (Ph.D.) from Université Laval, Québec-City/Canada (2001).

He is also a graduate of the Ecole Nationale des Services du Trésor in Paris/France (1964) and holds a degree in French - History from the Institut Supérieur Pédagogique in Kisangani (1972).

The writing of 'L'histoire de l'Eglise Anglicane du Congo' stems from the author's deep desire to provide the church with a work capable of reaching the general public.

This book is not only an account of the events that marked the establishment of the Anglican Church in the Congo, but also a source of knowledge for those interested in Anglicanism.

Apart from its documentary value, it traces the history of the Anglican Church in the Congo from its origins to the present day. It is well worth reading, and is an indispensable tool for researchers and others wishing to enrich their knowledge.

Printed by Books on Demand GmbH, Norderstedt / Germany